The Origin and Destiny of Life

The Origin and Destiny of Life

DISCOVER HOW THE EVIDENCE FROM SCIENCE, ARCHAEOLOGY & PROPHECY CONFIRMS THE ACCURACY OF THE BIBLE

DR E. K. VICTOR PEARCE

B.Sc. (Hons.) (UCL), Dip. Anth. (Oxon) M.R.E., D.Ed., F.R.A.I., C.F.

eagle

Guildford, Surrey

British Library Cataloguing in Publication Data. A catalogue record for this book is available from the British Library.
First published in 1993 by Nuprint Limited. This edition revised and updated published by Eagle Publishing Ltd, PO Box 530, Guildford, Surrey GU2 4FH.

Unless otherwise indicated, biblical quotations are from the author's own translation from the original Hebrew or Greek manuscripts.

Text abridged from *Evidence for Truth: Science, Archaeology and Prophecy*. Original book edited by Caire Meikle and sub edited by Juliet Taylor. This version with additional new material edited by Sue Wavre.

Typeset by Eagle Publishing
Printed by Creative Print and Design
ISBN No: 0 86347 397 0

CONTENTS

ILLUSTRATIONS

INTRODUCTION

LIFE'S ORIGIN

The origins and destiny of life are topical subjects. Readers will be surprised at how much science and the Bible reveal about these.

There is much scientific background in the Bible which can only be accounted for if the author of the Bible is the Creator of the universe. In speaking of science, I mean that science which has general consensus of agreement arising out of empirical investigation, not changing theories.

Science now uses popular terms. In answer to the question 'How did we get here?' Oparin (a dedicated Marxist) replied that the first ingredients for life arose out of 'soupy seas' existing in the primeval earth. Dr L. Croft (lecturer in biological science) calls it the 'great soup myth'. The Soviet Union sold that idea to universities around the world by financing science books, so that 'Oparin succeeded in converting most of western society to his belief'. Scientists now believe that the early seas were not soupy.

The origins of life go further back than that. Out in space NASA's space probe found the first ripples of gravity and 'lumps in the primeval soup'. A scientist explained 'that's when the early universe gave a hiccup and we've just heard the echo'. It shows that all things were leading up to man, others have said, to give an earth small enough for his gravity strength, but stars large enough to make his heavier atoms.

Concerning the origin of man, popular terms are again used. The skeleton in Africa suggested as man's origins is not given the long Latin name, but called 'Lucy'.

Cosmic dust was baked in the high pressure cookers of the large hot stars, and scientists now say that man was made of the same dust as the earth. Does that echo a verse in the Bible, 'God made man of the dust of the earth'?

Tablets, mounds and pottery dug up from older civilisations confirm that all the biblical dates and history in the Bible are both factual and true. Above all, the Bible contains God's prophecies from creation onwards to our future history. God tells the prophets before each stage, all that is to happen, all that will happen and why. In this way God proves that he is unfolding a remarkable plan for the future happiness of the world and for you. This plan could have unfolded without suffering if mankind had not rebelled against God. But these purposes will be fulfilled even by suffering, especially the suffering of Jesus Christ.

THEY'VE FOUND THE HANDBOOK!

What a find it would be if an admirer could reproduce Sir Malcolm Campbell's racing boat – the one that sank to the depths of Lake Windermere – and could reproduce that wonderful craft.

There has been a similar find – the Human Genome. It's the handbook of instruction of how to make a human being. Sooner or later, I've no doubt, it will even be on disk, so that you can play back the instructions on how to make a human being. Indeed in the year 2003 we are expecting a final draft of the handbook.

But some are horrified, of course. What could this mean for the future human race? Will the future creation of man be in the hands of man? But an even bigger concern is that, until the handbook of instruction was discovered, it was even thought that the human being had come together by itself accidentally. Now that the handbook has been discovered and its contents worked out, it is more and more obvious that there must have been a Creator who wrote the handbook or put it on disk. Of course you will guess that I am talking about the DNA code. The scientists have discovered all the instructions and put them into a paged book.

I remember the joy that my son had when he found the handbook to his secondhand car. It had developed a fault, which was very puzzling, and as the car was old, there didn't seem to be much hope of finding the original instructions. But to his delight, he came upon the handbook, and he whooped with joy as he could now repair the frustrating defect. Why have these scientists printed out the human handbook? Because now they can correct the defects that have arisen in the body of a human being with reference to the handbook!

Where is this book? It is in the cells of your body, very small but the instructions would fill 50 encyclopaedias – actually they are more like a ribbon. The words are put in code on a double ribbon, so a better likeness would be a tape, which we put in a tape-recorder and play back what the tape has recorded. God's tape of the DNA code is meaningless to us unless it is put in to a machine, which interprets the code and plays it back. God has provided such a machine – the ribosome. It is astonishing that even now the handbook has been discovered some people are suggesting that it too came together by accident! It does seem that we have reached the point where you need more faith to be an atheist than you do to be a believer!

So remember this when you read various articles which have started to appear in the press and on television. Remember that right from the first chapter of the Bible, God says that he created by words, and what he said must be what is recorded in the DNA, the Human Genome. When you think of that, try to think of science in a new light.

GCTGTTCAACCACTAATAGGTAAGAAATCAT
TCCAGACCGCTTTGGCCTCTATTAAGCTCAT
AAGATGATTTCGATTTTCTGACGAGTAACAA
CTCGTCGCTGCGTTGAGGCTTGCGTTTATG
TTCCTGCTCCTGTTGAGTTTATTGCTGCCGT
TTCAAACGGCCTGTCTCATCATGGAAGGCG
TCGAGCGTCCGGTTAAAGCCGCTGAATTGT
ACACTGACGTTCTTACTGACGCAGAAGAAA
TGATGTAATGTCTAAAAGGTAAAAAACGTTC
GCGAGGTACTAAAGGCAAGCGTAAAGGCG

Fig 1. Human Genome
This is a quarter of a 'page' from 'The Book of Man' or the human genome.
From a slide given to the author by Dr C. Berry, the geneticist.

1 ORIGIN OF LIFE

What a false picture the public is getting about the origin of life! It has taken the cleverest of our scientists to discover the mechanisms of life, and a very high percentage of these believe that life was created. For example, a vital piece of life's mechanism was worked out by Professor Kreb of Oxford on what is called Kreb's cycle. He is a Bible believer. Another whose name is linked to the cell's origin and the mechanism of enzymes is Professor Malcolm Dixon, who was Head of the Enzyme Biology Department, Cambridge University. He also is a convinced Christian. There are many many more Bible believing scientists. Dr Crick, the Nobel Prize winner who, with Watson, discovered the structure of DNA, even though he said he was an atheist, quotes Salvador Dali at the head of his report: 'The announcement of Watson & Crick on the DNA code is for me the real proof of the existence of God.' Yet the general public are given the impression that science has disproved God.

All scientists have found that the basis of life is the cell. The cells make up the constituent parts of the bodies of all creatures – the heart, the liver, kidneys, blood. Plants also are composed of cells. The cell works like a computer, and this computer has messages typed into it, so to speak, by a code – the DNA code.

As you look at a computer, ask yourself – could it have come together by accident? The argument by some who get all the media coverage is that if the materials of which computers are made are around on the planets, the computers could gradually manufacture themselves by a long series of accidents selected by their surroundings. This is the assumption by those who talk of carbonates being found in some meteorites which have fallen to earth. Life is made up of carbon (among other materials), therefore, they argue, these materials must have been brought together into living computers – like cells – by a series of accidents. It is like saying that because there is aluminium in many soils, these materials must have been formed into a computer without a manufacturer – perhaps thrown together by earthquakes to make all those computers found in schools and offices.

But computers won't work unless there is one who has been trained to be computer literate and to type the message into the computer. Also, before those typists could type in the message they would have to have the technical instructions. These must be supplied by the manufacturer, so did there have to be a manufacturer of the cell?

There is still a further difficulty. In the living cell, the computer instructions are in code; therefore, this code has to be translated or interpreted before it can be obeyed. There are special machines to do this in the cell; they are called the ribosomes. These ribosomes not only interpret; they also have extra machinery to carry out the instructions and produce the parts that create the living creature.

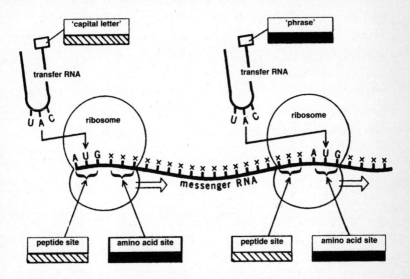

Fig 2. Machinery in our cells: Ribosomes and an RNA assembly line.
Both the 'capital letter' and the 'phrase' (methionine) are carried by a transfer-RNA that can plug into the code section (codon) AUG. However, the capital letter transfer-RNA can only fit into the peptide start point, while the phrase transfer-RNA can only fit into the amino acid site. When AUG occurs at the beginning of the messenger-RNA it first appears in the peptide start point, so the capital letter slots in. When the AUG code section occurs in the middle of the messenger, it first appears in the amino acid site, so that the phrase fits in.

Courtesy: C. Cheold What's Life? *BBC Publications*

2 LIFE

THE DNA GENETIC LIFE CODE

The order of events in creation is similar to that which science has discovered. Genesis says that it was the result of God's spoken word.

Each time God spoke, a new order of life came into being as a result of what he said. The DNA genetic code now reveals that all life forms are a result of a code of instructions recorded on chemical ribbons in the cells of all plants, animals and humans.

THE CELL

So let us look at the cell. I will make it simple because, even if you can master one or two points, you will be able to give them as powerful evidence for creation, because evidence from the cell is very convincing. On pages 26–28 you will see I have outlined (in a diagram and a summary) seven big problems about the cell which modern knowledge presents to one who does not believe in the Creator.

Even if you only master the first two points, they can floor an unbeliever unless they just will not face up to the facts. So don't think you have to digest all at once.

First there is the mystery of the origin of the workers on the production line. They are called enzymes. The enzyme which copied the Messenger RNA is created by that copy. It would not exist to copy unless there was an original Creator.

All the editor and sub-editor enzymes exist as a result of the editing. They would not be there to edit unless there was an original Creator.

The two hundred specialist workers in the cells of life are all made by the machinery they feed.

Then there is the mystery of the translator. Surely the one who knew the translation to put into the codebreaker, must be the same one who composed the DNA code, the Book of Man.

Dr François Jacob wrote, 'Life is no longer what is scrutinised in laboratories. Life is a language and a programme.' Dr George Beadle: 'It is a language as old as life itself; its words are buried deep in the cells of our bodies. It is the same language for all plants and animal life, including man.'

Since such quotations as these, it is now more widely known that the scientists of the world are deciphering the whole Book of Man. Some 8,000 scientists are on the job and the chromosomes are treated as books and the genes as chapters and gene clusters as paragraphs. Consequently, when identifying a particular place in the book, they quote book, chapter and verse and can detect where a faulty copying, for example, may have produced a disease.

CREATION: THE RESULT OF WORDS

It is the discovery that the creation of life is the result of words that has turned science upside down. As Michael Behe says in his recent book *Darwin's Black Box*, this is quite the reverse to what atheists expected. As Behe says,

> It was once expected that the basis of life would be exceedingly simple. That expectation has been smashed. An animal's vision, motion and other biological functions have proved to be no less sophisticated than television cameras and automobiles. Science has made enormous progress in understanding how the chemistry of life works, but the elegance and complexity of biological systems at the molecular level have paralysed science's attempts to explain their nature.

The knowledge that life is an organised cell as complex as any factory has confounded those who wanted to think that life originated in very simple ways.

They used to argue that it was a matter of something bringing the bits and pieces together accidentally, of particles and amino acids, which gradually got more and more complex. Science has now to start at the top end for origins, namely with the instructions in this factory of life – the DNA code. The atheists thought that the smallest parts required for life would come together by accident but now we discover that there is a whole code of instructions to bring together all the bits and pieces into a working factory and machine.

More and more scientists like Michael Behe have therefore questioned the theory of evolution.

CHECKPOINTS

MORE COMPLICATED THAN CLONING

1. **Still more mechanism is required. Why?**
   At this stage only a whole creature would be produced – cloned like Dolly the sheep, so the message would have to be divided up to produce specific parts – the liver, kidney or brain.

2. **For this there are editors and sub-editors.**
   These are enzymes, all of which have a specific job to do, selecting a paragraph or sentence of the DNA which manufactures a part for the living creature and gives a three-dimensional guide to where it is to go, otherwise you might have an ear growing on your elbow or your nose placed upside down, in which event you'd drown if you were caught in a shower of rain!

3. **Two big mistakes were made a hundred years ago.**
   They did not know that the cell was a highly technical factory, and that in this factory there were production lines governed by a code of instructions. The early microscopes were not powerful and the scientist only saw a cell with a blob in the middle that looked simple. Now the electron microscope magnifies up even the atoms. It shows that this production line is fed by enzyme workers, which feed in the parts on the assembly line.

4. **The discovery of the DNA code was a big surprise.**
   Scientists did not know that life was the result of words.

5. **Reality shows that all the parts of a living creature are assembled in obedience to very technical instructions.**
   This and much else makes the concept that life could happen by accident an impossible theory.

CHECKPOINTS

GOD'S AMAZING WORD-PROCESSOR

1. **Bible says God created by words.**
   DNA code demonstrates this, in Genesis 1, God speaks eight times (Ps 33:6,9; Ps 139:16; Heb 1:3; Col 1:15–17; Jn 1:1–3; Rev 22:13). Each time God spoke, a new order resulted. All life consists of cells which are operated by the DNA code.

2. **DNA instructions to man.**
   What Psalm 139:16 calls God's book (Authorised Version), is now called 'Book of Man' (Human Genome). Chromosomes = volumes; Gene clusters = chapters; Genes = sentences. Cystic fibros results from a copy error in book 11, chapter nine, paragraph 7, sentence 5. As many pages as 50 telephone directories are needed for all human instructions.

3. **In all cells of living creatures.**
   The cell is a computerised factory. A 'fax copier' takes instructions from the master hard copy. This (M.RNA) is sub-edited by eight sub-editors. They use God's genetic engineering enzymes, for tracing, cutting, rejoining and glueing. Edited copies (Transfer RNA) are used by workers (200 types) to feed into 20,000 translating machines (ribosomes). Only God could have known the translation.
   - Ribosomes obey instructions and produce protein chains.
   - These make body organs and tissues.
   - Code changed to alphabet of 64 'letters'.

4. **The sub-editors in the cell-machine**
   Seven or eight sub-editors take a portion of the tape which applies to the part of the body which they are responsible for producing.
   - They are each given their portion of tape by a messenger, RNA, who actually works to bring the portions of the DNA

to them, because the master tape is never allowed out of the central office. So, rather like a word processor, the messenger RNA makes copies of the master tape and brings the copies onto the workshop floor, first to the sub-editors, who take their section to translate it and to apply it to the various machines – the ribosomes.

- These are all allocated to their production lines; similar to a car production line where mechanics for that particular part are told their job in order to put the window frames into the car. In another area, on another production line, will be the cars having their wheels fitted and the assistant mates called co-enzymes screw on the nuts.
- What is the simile in the human body? It is that the workers, called enzymes, assisted by a workmate called a co-enzyme, take the material – the amino acids, and fit them together in the right order which, in turn, makes up the proteins which, in turn, make up, say, the heart or the liver.

5. **Mitochondrion fuel producer.**
To work cell's machinery.
Has female copyright and monopoly DNA.
Therefore scientists know that everybody is descended from one mother (Gen 3:20). 'Eve mother of all living.'

6. **Seven problems face the atheist.**
The code's origin, code breaker, fax copier, enzyme sub-editors, machine operators, the fuel factory, and meiosis (cell division). Each of these is interdependent upon the others. The factory has to be complete to work.

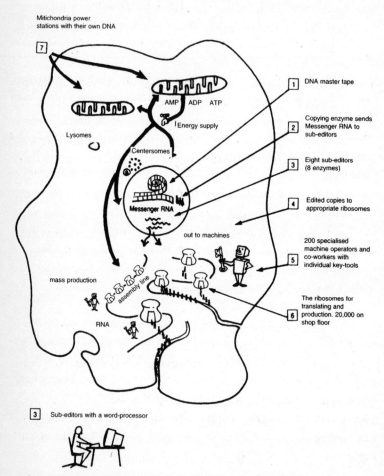

Mitichondria power
stations with their own DNA

AMP   ADP   ATP

Energy supply

Lysomes

Centersomes

Messenger RNA

out to machines

mass production

assembly line

RNA

1 DNA master tape

2 Copying enzyme sends
   Messenger RNA to
   sub-editors

3 Eight sub-editors
   (8 enzymes)

4 Edited copies to
   appropriate ribosomes

5 200 specialised
   machine operators and
   co-workers with
   individual key-tools

6 The ribosomes for
   translating and
   production. 20,000 on
   shop floor

3 Sub-editors with a word-processor

During gestation, cells are allocated certain jobs, i.e. specialised for liver, muscle, heart, etc. Only
a paragraph of the master tape is then used.

Fig 3. Cell's Automated Factory

CHECKPOINTS

EVIDENCE OF THE CREATOR
Here are the *seven big problems for the agnostic or atheist.*
Check each number with that on the cell drawing, Fig 3.

A. (No.1) The DNA code requires one million pages of instruction, gives complicated technical instructions to make an animal or man. They are more technical than any manmade computerised code to make an airliner etc. or any of the computers of the world – the brain is as complicated.
Comment: could a series of faults in instructions (mutations) make, by accident, such a technical code?

B. (No.6) This code needed someone who knew the translation and made a machine to translate it. It is called the ribosome.
Comment: someone was needed to know the code secret and make the code breaker.

C. (No.6) The ribosomes are on an assembly line to obey the decoded instructions and to produce the parts for the body. Complicated machines like the non-stop blood-pump (the heart) and the circulatory system of pipes to and from every organ. Some cells become the nerve system of the brain.
Comment: it needed technically complex and comparable machinery to read off instructions and to manufacture accordingly.

D. (No.4) Edited copies of the instructions are sent out to every ribosome. Sub-editors (No.3) with word-processors specialised to make either liver, muscle, heart, etc. The right sentence of instruction is selected to send to the ribosomes. These editors are made by the cell factory.
Comment: they are made by the cell, but the cell cannot make them until they are made, because they are part of its machinery.

E. (No.5) Two hundred different specialised workers, or enzymes, attend the production machines (ribosomes). These are all made by the cell factory.

Comment: Dr Francis Crick said that these were '200 frozen miracles'. The cell cannot make them unless they already exist to make them.

F. (No.7) The Fuel and Power department, or Mitochondria, supplies fuel for every working machine (organelle) in the cell. It supplies fuel in three grades—one star, two star and three star. This power station is as complicated as any made by man.

Comment: it needs the fuel it produces to start its own fuel producing machinery to make fuel. Who produced the first fuel?

G. When a cell itself has become specialised during gestation it becomes part of the brain, heart, or blood cell, etc. the centresomes (No.8) multiply it into those cells and it is directed to become part of that organ in the right part of the body.

Comment: who provided the three-dimensional blueprint for correct positioning?

So now we see that instead of the primitive idea that pieces of life could come together by accident, reality shows that all the parts of a living creature are assembled in obedience to very technical instructions. As I said before, this and much else makes the concept that life could happen by accident an impossible theory.

CHECKPOINTS

MORE ON DNA

1. Sometimes people are deceived by such terms as 'the instructions were contained in the DNA molecule', the word 'molecule' gives the impression that it was some simple single unit of matter, because it has been put into a simple term. But:
   - that so-called molecule is now a library which, as Dr Francis Crick says, would need 4,000 books of 500 pages long to contain all the information. Or, in other words, to be 65 times longer than all Shakespeare's works and 35 times longer than the *Encyclopaedia Britannica*. That is the length of the DNA code which has the instructions to create a human being and, indeed, similar lengths are required to create any of the animals.
   - if even one word gets wrongly copied, that causes a major mutation or disease. Couple this with the fact that this information, the DNA code, is upon two ribbons.
2. There is also a further difficulty in accounting for this creative information. Even if one could explain that all this technical instruction could come together by accident, it would be of no use in the cell factory unless it was translated and so there are as many as 15,000 or 20,000 ribosomes. These ribosomes are there to
   - translate the instructions, otherwise they would be meaningless. Instructions on the tapes run through the centre of the ribosome in a similar manner to a cassette tape which has to be placed in a machine for anybody to hear what is on the tape. It would seem reasonable to suggest that the one who created the ribosome would also need to be the one who knew the language and translation for the DNA code.

CHECKPOINTS

CREATED LIFE

There are more difficulties for the one who wants to disprove creation. The DNA code says how all the parts of a person or animal or plant should come together. DNA, as you will know, stands for Deoxyribonucleic acid, which refers to the materials on which the instructions are put. The word 'acid' is deceiving because actually it is a double ribbon upon which the instructions are put – rather like a tape-recorder ribbon.

How to translate the code.
The translator would have to know the translation. Now in all living things there is provided a machine to translate the code, to obey its instructions and to produce the article (the ribosome). Without the translator, even the code would be useless. Obviously, there must be an important link between the originator of the code instructions and however the translating machine was provided. I can only see the answer being that it was the one and same person, namely the creator. Furthermore, the ribosome has to obey the instructions and produce the goods described.

It becomes obvious that the elements of life could not fall together by accident anywhere in the universe, on any planet, unless God had created it and produced the machinery. So the question constantly asked in the papers 'Is there life elsewhere?' is answered by the reply 'Only if God created it.'

3 JUST CHANCE?

I was debating this subject at a Students Union in Birmingham University in the year 2000. It was a friendly discussion and I had said that to suggest that all the mechanism of a living cell could come together by accident was as unlikely as a motor car assembling itself. Even given an immense course of time would the parts come together correctly; the batteries, then the spark plugs, then the dynamo, then the fuel system, carburettor, fuel pumps etc? All the parts had to be complete before the car would work.

Let us parallel a cell's mechanism with that of a car, even though science has now found that the cell's basic machinery of life is more complicated. In addition, it is seen that all the cells' components have to be complete before life could arise. A car would not work while still waiting for the accidental arrival of the fuel department. (In the cell this is the mitochondrion.) It would not work while waiting for the production line mechanics (machine operators with their own special key to start their machine, called the enzymes and co-enzymes). It would not work while waiting for the DNA instructions to the cell factory to get the production line moving. It could not wait millions of years until the code breakers (the ribosomes) found how to translate the DNA instructions for which '200 frozen miracles' were required, in the words of Dr Francis Crick, the Nobel Prize winner. Frozen, because they all had to be there instantly for the machinery to work.

I was giving these parallels, when a group of young men took me up on this illustration. They disputed my illustration of the car. They said the history of the car was also one of gradual development. First, there were horse-drawn wagons, then horseless carriages, then the crude-looking horseless carriage was replaced by the primitive motor car, which was developed into today's highly efficient limousine.

Can you see the obvious reply to this?

CHECKPOINTS

THE REPLY

1. **Each stage was the result of intelligent, creative planning** by human beings! Also, their inventions had to be put together piecemeal by creative man. Then factories were built, working like the living cell. The factory also had to be designed and built by inventive human beings. Their argument seemed to reinforce the creation model.

2. Science has moved on to an entirely different picture. Those early atheists thought they were accounting for the existence of a living creature itself, but they now find that **life is produced by a factory, and secondly that the factory is guided by recorded instructions** – the DNA tape. The scene has switched from the car itself to the factory and the manager's instructions.

3. A body – its heart, liver, kidneys, brain, etc., is made up of proteins, which are constructed amino acids. It takes between 100 and 1,000 amino acids (think of dominoes with right numbers on them) to be placed together in the right succession. Atheist evolutionists first worked on the possibility of millions of the constituents required coming together in the required order by accident. Then having got that right accidental pattern, **a self-replicating machine to repeat it forever afterwards.**

4. **Then science discovered that there was a factory putting together that living piece of life** – namely the cell – and further a coded computer had highly technical instructions typed into the DNA.

5. **Then it was discovered that there were code breakers** – thousands of them – to code-break the messages into technical instructions – a normal cell factory had 15,000 code breakers to translate the instructions.

6. In the remarkable programme *The Codebreakers of Station X*, a war secret kept for 50 years was revealed. It took 3,000 codebreakers (Wrens) to use code-breaking machines to interpret German secret messages (German machines spinning cogged wheels used different letters every time the notches whirred). (By breaking the code they were able to notify Monty's desert army of every move which Rommel was to take and then where Grand Admiral Karl Doenitz' submarines were going to torpedo Atlantic convoys, which were preparing for the Allies' invasion of the Continent; 3,000 Wren code-breakers!) But **who supplied the code-breakers in the cells factory?**

7. The code-breakers in the cells are called ribosomes. They also have attendants to each machine, like 3,000 Wrens with 200 different tools. This was what assembled the amino acids in proteins into hearts, muscles, nerves and blood veins – **not by a series of accidents.**

CHECKPOINTS

HAVE THE EVOLUTIONISTS ATTEMPTED TO ACCOUNT FOR THIS?

1. Michael Behe has looked through hundreds of books, theses and experiments and not one attempt to account for the origin of the factory, the code, or the codebreakers, or the 200 codebreakers' special tools, has been found.

2. Is this because they know they are beyond explanation without a Creator?

3. 'There has never been a meeting, or a book, or a paper on details of the evolution of complex biochemical systems' (M. Behe, *Darwin's Black Box*, p 179).

4. Behe then refers, on page 182, to biochemistry textbooks – in their reference to evolution never once do they refer to the main evidence against it, i.e. the origin of the factory, the origin of the code or the origin of the code-breakers.

5. Evolutionists are very clever at switching from proper science to barrister-like skilled arguments, e.g. Stephen Dawkin switches the argument from the impossibility of cars being made by scrap iron, bolts and rubber accidentally flying together into a motor car to the possibility of a car ignition switch being accidentally switched on by the right key randomly chosen. The public don't see that he has switched attention from the main problem of origin of the car to a tool already created!

6. But what does this do? It switches attention from the job of proper empirical science, which would give an accurate assessment, to depend upon the skill of the debaters. Those trained as barristers know that if they are losing a case they are advised

to bring in a red herring, which has nothing to do with the real evidence. It is amazing how skilled they are at doing this and how easily Christians are side-tracked.

7. Evolutionists need to forsake trying to explain how amino acids formed into proteins and proteins into hearts and blood vessels (i.e. how they came together), and start to explain the existence of the production mechanism, i.e:
   • the code with its technical instructions
   • the code-breakers to translate the instructions
   • the production line to obey the instructions
   • the factory of the cell which puts the car together.

SCIENCE AND TRUTH

The most effective way for you to give evidence to a doubter is to use what science already accepts in the order of creation. Then reveal to him that this correlates with Genesis 1. How did it then get into the Bible in a non-scientific age unless God revealed it?

I quote scientists to show how new facts are bringing leading scientists back to acceptance of the Creator, and that science shows that mankind was the object of his creation. Scientists call this the 'Anthropic Principle'.

Many doubters have been surprised when I have shown them the British Museum book, *The Succession of Life through Geological Time*, by Oakley and Muir-Wood. I have put the chapter and verses of Genesis down the margin of this science book. The reader can see that the order of events is the same; green vegetation to supply oxygen, life in the waters, land animals and finally mankind.

Dr Rendle Short made this comment in his book, *Modern Discovery and the Bible:*

These considerations bring to light a perfectly amazing accordance between the Creation narrative and the discoveries of modern science. When we remember the wild guesses as to the ultimate nature and origin of the earth that were current amongst other ancient people, the accuracy of Genesis stands out in solitary grandeur. Geology is a young science; the classification of strata is not much older than a hundred years; we may be sure the author of the Creation narrative derived none of his information from fossil hunting. Neither guesswork nor intuition taught the writer to arrange events in the correct order. This narrative bears the marks of a divine inspiration.

For the timing of creation events see Chapter 9.

CHECKPOINTS

CORRELATION OF SCIENCE AND SCRIPTURE

(By giving the order of events, we do not necessarily substantiate the timescale sometimes suggested.)

Science	Genesis *Chapter 1*
Before the days of Creation	
The universe begins with the explosion of the primeval atom	'In the beginning God created the heavens and the earth' v 1
'Streams of light quanta from . . . the Big Bang' (Gamov)	'Let there be light' v 3
Our galaxy begins to rotate	
Pre-Cambrian Eras	
Earth swaddled in thick steamy bands	1st Day begins in darkness v 5
Condensation into oceans and clouds	2nd Day 'Let an expanse separate the waters from the waters' v 6
Early Pre-Cambrian Schists with rocks oxidised by chloroplasts and blue-green algae	3rd Day land emerges v 9 'Let the earth bring forth green' (*deshe*) v 11
Dense vapours clear to reveal sun, moon and stars	4th Day 'Let there be lights in the sky' v 14 'God had already made the sun, moon and stars' v 16
Post-Cambrian Eras	
Marine fossils swarm the strata	5th Day 'Let the waters bring forth swarms of life' v 20
Insects and angio-sperms	'Winged creatures' v 20b
Amphibians and Reptiles	'Great sea monsters' v 21
New Life Eras	
Land animals Age of mammals	6th Day 'Let the earth bring forth living creatures'
Man	6th Day, latter part, 'Let us make man'

4 LUMPS IN THE PRIMEVAL SOUP

There was great excitement among the scientists when the NASA space probe sent back pictures of the first ripples in the universe. 'Wow! What an exciting discovery,' said one scientist from Durham. What caused those ripples? It was the force of gravity. Scientists use funny language; they said, 'There were lumps in the primeval soup!' Yes, that is how they put it – 'lumps in the primeval soup'! And do you know what some of them then said?

> The strength of gravity shows that it was intended to lead up to man. Man was in mind. Why? Because 'the strength of gravity was just the right strength for the size of the earth to support man'. Dr Nigel Calder said, 'For man to walk on this planet with 12,000 kilometres of the earth beneath his feet, man had to have the two gravity balances in his head rightly tuned.'

Many scientists call this 'The Anthropic Principle'. Isaiah 45:12 puts this principle in a nutshell. I quote, 'God said, "I made the earth and created man upon it." ' Those first ripples had man in mind. It was written into the space–time plan!

LEADING SCIENTISTS CONFIRM THE BIBLE

Is this the word that God spoke when he said, 'Let there be light'? Two leading world scientists say it is. Le Maitre, the mathematician who first worked it all out, said this: ' "Let there be light" correctly described the origin of the universe.' Another leading physicist, Professor Geoge Gamov, said that the Divine command, 'Let there be light!' was completely scientific. Here are his words: 'All the chemical elements which we deal with today must have been formed within the first 30 minutes of the life of this universe, and it accords with the Divine command, "Let there be light". There certainly was light through this intense radiation.'

These two scientists knew that there were two verses **before** the words 'Let there be light' (the Big Bang?). They refer to the origin of the universe: 'In the beginning God created the heavens (universe) and the earth.'

The dust which later became the earth, was 'without form and void'!

There is **no** date given to 'the beginning'.

Moses, who wrote these words, hints in the psalm which he wrote – Psalm 90 – that before the mountains and the earth were formed, God's days were great lengths of time. 'A thousand years are but a section of the night.'

As these days in Genesis 1 refer to days before the sun, it may raise the question of how long those days were and so Moses' Psalm 90 would guide us.

NASA SPACECRAFT DISCOVERY

I stated before that many secular scientists are now admitting that the way matter and gravity were formed in the early universe indicates that it had man in mind. This is, of course, what the Bible says.

Since the discovery of the ripples in outer space by the NASA probe, people are asking, 'Why are the scientists so excited about this discovery in the universe?'

Well, it was to the American Physical Society meeting, early in 1992, that the satellite discovery was presented.

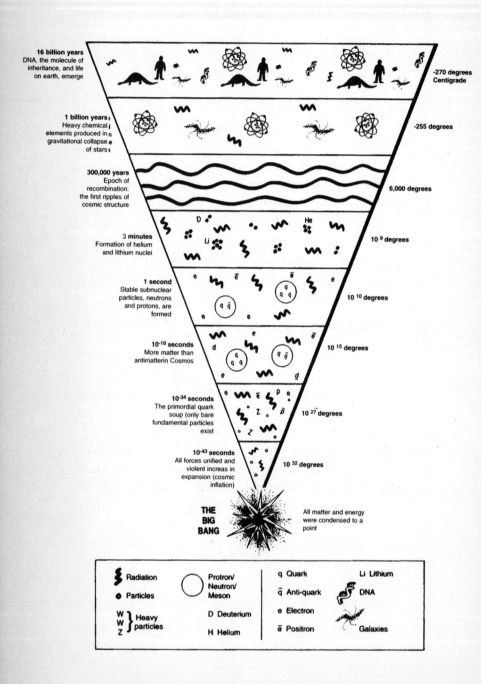

Fig 4. The Big Bang theory.

Courtesy: The Independent

QUARK SOUPS IN SIX FLAVOURS

I like the popular cookery terms the scientists used about the thin gruel at the beginning of creation coalescing into a lumpy soup soon after creation. This space probe gave the first evidence that it had actually happened. Dr Michael Turner said the discovery was, 'The Holy Grail of Cosmology'. The satellite had sent back pictures of the ripples which were forming into matter. The Bible adds that it was God who was doing it.

Another scientist asks, 'But how did the lumps get into the porridge?' – to use a different culinary term. The matter of which the earth – and your body – is made, was formed by gravity pulling together all kinds of primary particles. Science has been finding that matter is more complex than anyone thought. At one time, matter was thought to consist only of protons, electrons and neutrons, but this soup, as the analogist has called it, consists of lots of simpler elements called quarks. What that satellite has discovered is the formation of quark soup to make up the material needed for galaxies and planets of life.

There are 36 different kinds of quarks in the universe's quark soup with interacting forces to hold things together. There are up quarks, down quarks, charmed quarks, strange quarks, top quarks and bottom quarks. All these in turn have anti-quarks, anti-ups, downs, tops and bottoms and so on. This is all to keep matter from falling apart. Do you remember what Colossians 1:17 says, that 'God created all things by Jesus by whom all things hold together'?

CHECKPOINTS

NASA SPACE PROBE

1. **NASA feedback** was like a video run backwards catching up with the beginning of the universe. Revelation 20:11 describes a 'Big Bang', but God causes it. Gamov and Le Maitre who worked it out, quoted Genesis 1:3 'Let there be light'.
Scientists use culinary terms:
   - First elementary particles were like 'thin gruel'.
   - 'Ripples' proved gravity operating (lumps in the quark soup).
   - 'Universe hiccuped and NASA heard the echo.'

2. **Man-centred: strength of gravity proved man was in mind**
   - Anthropic principle – required small earth but big stars. Why? Any planet bigger than earth would crush man. Yet huge stars were needed to fuse the quarks into atoms, required for man's body. These novae stars then exploded the dust into space for man's body (and planets).
   - Professor Calder (BBC science broadcaster) says, 'Gravity detectors in man's head' . . . are rightly adjusted for earth's mass. Anthropic principle supported by leading scientists. 'I made the earth and created man upon it' (Is 45:12).
   - DNA acids for man created in the hot interiors of exploding stars. St John was overawed that he had touched the 'Word of Life' (1 Jn 1:1).

3. **Reality is invisible** Scientists find that what is detectable in the whole universe is only 1%. The other 99% is invisible. 'The worlds were framed by the activating word (*hreemati*) of God, so that the things which are seen were not made by the visible' (Heb 11:3).
Stephen Hawking of Cambridge is attempting to combine Quantam Physics with Relativity to give a Theory of Everything. He wonders whether we shall know everything

without the mind of God.

Solution: the mind of God is given in his Word (Heb 1:1).

Note: Quantam Physics

Primary elements are 36 quarks in 6 flavours and 3 colours.

Relativity is $E = mc^2$

* * * * * * * * * *

In addition to new updating, this book is a digest of the three books by Dr Victor Pearce in the *Evidence for Truth* series on Science, Archaeology and Prophecy. *The Origin and Destiny of Life* makes a convenient handbook of evidence easy to use. When a fuller explanation is needed, the original volumes may be consulted.

5 Fossils

IMAGINARY STOOPING APEMEN

What picture does the discovery of more fossils give in regard to so-called apemen? The trend in manlike skeletons is to show that there were no apemen links between true man and the ape. This may surprise you because of all the propaganda which you get. For example, in Amsterdam, I saw posters showing apemen gradually walking more and more upright. In actual fact, no such skeletons have been found.

Fig. 5. Row of stooping 'apes'.
Showing the false speculation by Richard Leakey in a series of stooping hominids which never existed but which are often depicted in school text books.

An article written in the *New Scientist* actually laments this fact. It is written by Dr M. Pickford of Oxford. He takes evolution for granted, only lamenting that, as regards man, there is no evidence to support it. He says: 'The fossil void is particularly frustrating because it was during this time that the earliest human ancestor embarked on a vital stage in its journey towards humanity.' The fossil void he speaks of is the absence of apemen. But that is what begs the whole question.

POWERFUL FOSSIL EVIDENCE

Some have asserted that the succession of fossils in the rocks has been falsely concocted on an evolutionary assumption. This is not correct. The fossil record was discovered by geologists a long time before Darwin launched his theory.

Indeed, the fossil record was evidence against evolution. Even Darwin acknowledged this!

For Christians, untrained in geology, to attack the fossil record is like shooting themselves in the foot and making themselves ineffective for battle.

CHECKPOINTS

MISSING MISSING LINKS
Science supports Genesis' order of life's appearance:

1. But each order appears suddenly. Are there any links? Darwin admitted that unless links were found, the fossils supported a series of special creations.

   Those links have not been found. Fossil scientists, Coffin and Anderson, say, '. . . even more like creative acts than in Darwin's day. Not gaps in fossil records found, only absence of link fossils.'

2. Six new theories have been presented by scientists: explosive evolution; saltation leaps; reptile lays bird's egg; hopeful monster theory; neo-Darwinism by mutations; punctuated equilibria.

3. Mendel's genetics also brought in a new problem for Darwinism. Darwin thought a trait attained in life could be passed to offspring. But genetics show that only characteristics in the genes were inherited.

4. Imaginary apemen.

   Fictional drawings abound. All are either quadrapeds or upright walkers.

   Meet Lucy 'Beginning of humankind'.

   Fossil void between ape and man was lamented by Johanson and Edey who found 'Lucy', and by Dr M. Pickford.

5. Don't shoot yourself in the foot. Make fossils your friend. Some Christians dump good evidence. Geological succession was discovered 50 years before Darwin. Overlaps explain why some fossil orders are reverse.

THE ABSENCE OF LINK FOSSILS

Today, many scientists are having a re-think, and in any case the old Darwinian model has been greatly modified by two factors. Firstly, our knowledge of Mendel's genetics and Crick's DNA demonstrates that nothing can happen in a species which does not happen in its DNA genes. Secondly, it has become plain that new and higher orders appear in groups comparatively suddenly. Consequently, some have called it 'explosive evolution', a seeming contradiction in terms.

It would be better to associate these appearances with each of the times that God spoke the creative words. In other words, such complicated creatures were the result of re-coding of DNA, the language of life, when the dramatically advanced orders appear, such as vertebrates, amphibians, reptiles, birds, mammals and man.

LIFE APPEARS SUDDENLY

The overall picture is that of a series of jumps to major new types of animals. It is not now sufficient to excuse ourselves by saying that we merely need to look for more fossils. That has been done, yet the picture is the same.

This is really a death blow to Darwinism, and so evolutionary scientists have come up with a succession of alternatives. There have been five new theories all succeeding each other, because none of them is satisfactory even to evolutionists.

Professor Sir Fred Hoyle and Professor C. Wickramasinghe, eminent Cambridge scientists, reflect the change: 'Contrary to Darwin's theory . . . evolution on earth was a series of leaps.' The fossil picture gives a pattern of the major groups of new advanced animals appearing together. Between them and their assumed ancestors, there is a lack of linking fossils to show evolutionary progress. This is a consistent story throughout the fossil record.

THE MIRACLE OF SIGHT AND FLIGHT

Did your camera fall from heaven, already complete with batteries and film?

Did your TV set come together accidentally through a storm sweeping into your house or was it a hurricane which blew all the components together with the screws in place?

A man on television said that this was possible concerning the eye, the human eye. It could all have come together. How? By a series of a million accidents selected by environment.

Actually, your camera and TV set are very simple compared with the complexity of the human eye. The automatic focusing of the camera is simple compared with the very much finer focusing of your iris and lens. The little colour spots on your TV screen only number a few thousand. Compare that with the retina at the back of your eye. Your eye has 20 million nerve endings taking the message of sight to your brain. Yes, 20 million! Your TV set can only read the signals from the studio by a rapid shut off and on system to simulate a succession of still shots. Your brain has a similar mechanism to read the moving picture.

Did God intend man to use the telescope and microscope to explore his universe? I believe he did because the human eye has a very sensitive area in the centre of the back of the eye. It is called the fovea and in the middle of that is an even more sensitive area called the macula. It is so fine and full of communication nerves that it can read the smallest image. Without these, we would know little about the universe or the genes of inheritance in the DNA code. Even more marvellous is the creation of all this each time a child is conceived, because the instructions for it are contained in the cell's genetic code.

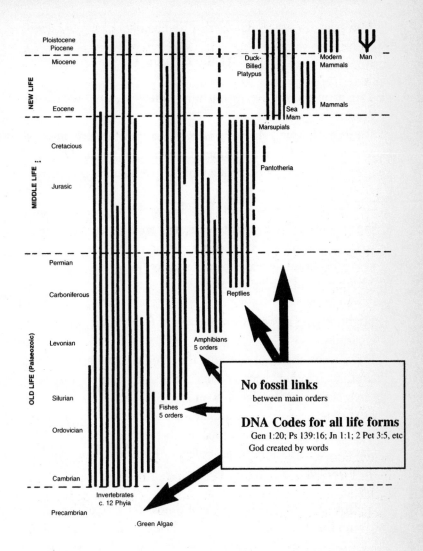

Fig. 6. Fossil record of life, showing the sequence in which the seven main orders of life appear.

Each vertical line represents a creature in the fossil record and shows the period it was/is extant.

Victor Pearce does not necessarily commit himself to the time scales usually given. The succession of fossils are those generally agreed by palaeontologists. This succession is similar to Genesis 1, but it was when God spoke that a new order came into being, not by evolution. The rocks show no link fossils between the main orders of life, so the supposed evolutionary branches have been omitted from the diagram.

CHECKPOINTS

THE GREAT TV COVER-UP

1. **TV propaganda for evolution hides present scientists' doubts.**

   Rocks are barren before the *sudden creation* of twelve phyla of marine life in Cambrian times. Darwin admitted in *Origin of Species* Chapter 10 that they looked like separate acts of creation.

   As Genesis 1:20 says, 'God said, "Let waters swarm with moving creatures" '. David Attenborough on TV said there must have been soft-bodied creatures earlier which left no fossils. But soft bodies *do* leave fossils. Sea urchins of the Cambrian period are still similar today.

2. **Flight. Flying aeronautical marvels of four different kinds of creatures.**

   Even according to evolution, they could not have evolved from each other, because they belong to entirely different phyl, classes, orders, families and species.

   Dr David Buckley congratulates the author on: 'Your excellent example of flight, animals with flight are in 2 phyla, 4 classes, 28 insect orders, 32 orders of birds and 1 or 2 orders of mammals.'

   Yet

   • BBC 2 in May 2000 spoke of dinosaurs developing wings (no fossil record of it). *Encyclopaedia Britannica* says they 'practised swift runs and leaps for thousands of years until they could fly'!!

   • But birds are of 32 unrelated orders. They have unique mechanisms of interlocking feathers, which are quite different from reptilian scales.

   • Insects are in almost 20 unrelated orders. Evolution cannot explain their metamorphosis in a cocoon. When they first appeared some were trapped in amber. Just the same as modern insects.

- Bats are like mammals with wings – no fossils of mice changing into bats.

There is no evolutionary record of any of these. Professor Fred Hoyle found Archaeopterix to be a fraud, with feathers glued on. What of the other six fossils? *New Scientist* found they had no feathers!

God created every winged creature (Gen 1:21).

God created the peacock's wings (Job 39:13).

Migration of birds by God's wisdom (Job 39:26).

3. **Sight:** from first fossils, all have eyes, even worms:

Sonic sight for bats (dark caves).

Telescopic sight for eagles.

Trilobites had complex eye for opaque deep water.

Octopus eyes like human's (yet entirely different phyla).

'He who made the eye, shall he not see?' (Ps 94:9)

Human eye: 20 million nerves from retina to brain.

Automatic focusing and light metre of iris and lens.

Twenty-two British Museum biologists said in 1981, 'Evolution is not a fact.'

6 THE FRAUDS OF EVOLUTION
CALL MY BLUFF

A favourite programme on television for some time has been *Call My Bluff*. As you may know, there are two teams of three people and each team tries to deceive the other on the meaning of a very old word taken from *The Oxford English Dictionary*. Each member of the team gives his own highly convincing description of the word and then the opposing team has to decide which is the correct meaning. The explanations are so convincing that the opposing team find it very difficult to hit on the right one.

There is a similar kind of game enacted concerning the theory of evolution. The trouble is that on the whole there is no opposing team allowed to expose all the erroneous assumptions of those propagating evolution, although many of us scientists have asked to be given the space on television in order to reveal the errors. It is for this reason that so large a percentage of the population is deceived into thinking that the theory of evolution is proved. In actuality more and more scientists are now questioning it because the use of better microscopes and telescopes and a larger balance of information has called the whole theory into question.

Also there is another element which has deceived the public. A writer in the *New Scientist* magazine asked, 'Why is it that so many frauds have become a characteristic of the theory of evolution?' I propose to speak about these frauds, but first of all let me list them.

1. **Misleading Drawings** of supposed ape-men and stooping ape-men, Haeckel's drawings of the supposed evolution recap

of the embryo in the womb, Dawn Man tooth, Java Man.

2. **The Long Suspension List** – which is kept from the public because it doesn't fit with the current evolutionary theory.

3. **The Cave Man Disappearances** – e.g. the disjunction between Neanderthal Man & modern Homo Sapiens.

4. **Archaeopteryx.**

5. **The Fraudulent Re-assemblage of Human Fossils** – such as the Piltdown Skull.

6. **The Fossil Succession Frauds**. e.g. concerning graptolites and trilobites.

7. **The Primeval Soup Fraud** – concerning the origin of life.

It was in connection with Ernst Haeckel's fraudulent drawings

Fig. 7. Cartoon of Charles Darwin showing prevailing humour in the mid-nineteenth century.

Courtesy: Punch Magazine

that the writer in *New Scientist* expressed surprise that there were so many frauds associated with the theory of evolution. The *New Scientist* printed the information concerning Haeckel as being condemned by the German universities and sentenced for fraudulent drawings of the embryo. He confessed to drawing from memory and was convicted of fraud at the University of Jena (*New Scientist*, 6 September 1997). Perhaps at this stage we should go through the other list of drawings.

CHECKPOINTS

DECEPTIONS

1. The **Dawn Man** tooth – this tooth was unearthed and declared to be a very important link between ape and man and was printed in a number of science publications and books. Four years later, it was re-examined and found to be the tooth of a pig! The books hastily erased reference to it, but there was one book that did not do so, and was unaware of the correction.

2. The **Java Man** – discovered by Dubois, a Dutch anthropologist. He was always drawn looking more ape than man with a pronounced stoop. When the theory changed 20 years later and re-classed the ape man as Homo-erectus, upright walking, it was then revealed that he had hidden the thigh bones under the floorboards of his house, and that they were from an upright walking Homo. Similarly with other discoveries such as that of Lucy. At first she was depicted as walking with a stoop, but following examination of the leg bones revealed that she was also upright walking. As she was regarded as the earliest Homo species, it meant that there were no specimens now who were half stooping, i.e. no specimens between the stooping ape and the upright walking man.

3. Evolutionists were not deterred and said that we do not need any evidence of the transitory period between the ape and man, because we know the theory must be correct.

    i. Dr Martin Pickford laments the lack of fossil evidence for this vital stage. He calls it the fossil void. He wrote in the *New Scientist:* 'The fossil void is particularly frustrating because it was during this time that the earliest human ancestor embarked on a vital stage of its journey towards humanity.'

    ii. Don Johanson in his firm faith in evolution felt that evidence was not necessary! Likewise with no fossils for the in-between time, he finds it easy to picture the process. 'We picture evolution starting with a primitive ape-like type that generally over a long period of time, began to be less and less ape-like and more man-like. There was no abrupt cross-over,' he adds confidently 'from ape to human, but probably a rather fuzzy time of in-between types. We have no fossils to tell us what went on during that in-between time.'

    iii.Richard Leakey writes in his book, 'We will only know when we find evidence of the very first bi-pedal apes.'

    iv.The lack of evidence for what they call this vital period does not disturb R. L. Johanson either, he also confesses, 'We have no fossil yet that tell us what went on during the in-between time'. By the in-between time he means the vital supposed ape-man period when it is assumed that quadrupedal knuckle walking apes gradually walked upright

4. It will be remembered that Richard Leakey drew pictures of ape-men gradually walking upright which were displayed throughout the world and on television. As you see, the above are confessions that no such specimens have ever been found. In a later book Richard Leakey has some fresh drawings for us, showing the ape gradually descending from the trees and thus forced to walk upright to run across grass-

lands. Again there are no indications of the human skeleton of any such past history. Other theories on what made Homo walk upright are still propagated. Sir Alister Hardy suggested that it was when Homo trod water to get oysters at the seaside that in stooping and bending and returning to upright, his bones gradually changed for upright walking position. There is still another suggestion . . .

5. It will be noticed that all these theories are just plausible suggestions and it is this kind of argument which has been taken as science when in actuality the scientific method has not been followed at all.

6. It should also be remembered that Dr Manchip-White in the Universities Library series on evolution says that a characteristic of the research is a long suspension list of skulls ignored because they did not fit in with the contemporary theory of succession. Recently, a series on BBC1 spoke of the abrupt disappearance of Neanderthal Man in the cave records. It endeavoured to show they didn't disappear abruptly, but that there must have been a merging period into modern Homo sapiens.

7. Actually all the cave records do not show this. There are about 20 caves in Europe and the Near East which show that **Neanderthal Man** disappeared entirely and that modern Homo sapiens appeared in the cave records a long time after that disappearance. It is not acceptable to evolutionists to acknowledge this and so they look to the caves in Palestine where they think it could be shown that Neanderthal Man from other parts of the world migrated into Europe through Palestine. These were at Mount Carmel, the Skhul Cave and the Tabun Cave.

8. However, these caves were re-examined by D.R. Brothwell and E. Higgs and it was shown that there was the same hia-

tus of a long period when the Neanderthals disappeared and Homo sapiens began. ('The People of Mt. Carmel', D.R. Brothwell, *Proceedings of the Prehistoric Society* 27:155, 1961 & 'Some Pleistocene Faunas of the Mediterranean Coastal Areas', E. Higgs, *Proceedings of the Prehistoric Society* 25:44 1961). This was largely forgotten until I pointed it out to an Oxford scientist and told him of the records, about which he knew nothing.

It is typical to forget anything that does not fit in the evolution theory, because to admit that there was this hiatus when Neanderthals disappeared and Homo sapiens suddenly appeared, would mean there is no evolutionary connection. The explanation would be that the Homo sapiens was a new creation from a Creator or that a separation was due to a catastrophe similar to the one that destroyed the dinosaurs.

9. On that TV programme mentioned in point 6 it was said that there was evidence that only Homo sapiens buried their dead with ceremony and that this revealed a consciousness of spiritual things. This again is not correct because in Chappelle aux Saints cave, a cross section of it reveals a Neanderthal burial in which the skeleton occurs with a slab over it showing that it was buried with ceremony. The same kind of evidence comes from the well-known cave near Iran.

10. **Archaeopteryx** is the fossil of a pre-historic bird, the first to have feathers on its fossil and was referred to by David Attenborough during a three-day weekend evolution propaganda series for three hours a night during 1998. He did not appear to know that it was claimed to be a fraud. Professor Fred Hoyle had re-examined the specimen fossil and found that the feathers had been stuck on with glue. Somebody must have told David Attenborough after his programme so in a later programme he mentioned this and said 'but there are several other fossils of archaeopteryx which were found in Germany'. It seemed that that was a convincing reply until I

happened to notice in *New Scientist* that none of the other fossils had feathers on them. You will remember that I referred to the programme *Call My Bluff*; it is unfortunate that nobody was allowed by David Attenborough to call his bluff.

11. The fact that there's no evidence that Neanderthal migrated into Europe through the Palestine bridge between the continents removes the theory. A very dogmatic series on BBC2 in the year 2000 did not mention that many scientists were not agreed that the early Homos were from Africa, but that they came from the Near East and moved into Africa later. This is typical of such programmes that any other opinion by scientists is completely ignored. Actually the Royal Anthropological Society sent geneticists to take samples from all the races around the world to see what their origin was and genetically they were shown to come from one origin – which migrated from the Garden of Eden so that all races whether from Africa, China or America are all descended from the Near East. For this reason Richard Leakey in a later book has said that scientists are divided between an Eden origin and a Noah's three children origin.

12. The **Piltdown Skull** was discovered in 1912 at Piltdown in Sussex. It was reported as an important missing link between apes and man. Then in 1952, forty years later, leading anthropologists re-examined the specimen because it no longer fitted in with the current theory. It was discovered that the skull top was only 400 years old and had come from a Saxon grave. The shattering revelation was that the jaw fitted to it was that of an ape, the teeth had been filed and stained with chromate to make them look ancient and the jaw filed to fit in with the skull. The leading Professor W. E. Gros Clark says 'It was a most skilful forgery' it must have been done by a trained anthropologist and 'it had been deliberately faked to give it a fossilised appearance' (*History*

of the Primates, W. E. Gros Clark, British Museum).

13. The textbook for schools written by Dr Morley Davies, *An Introduction to Palaeontology* is also typical of how school textbooks present a false picture for children and students. In it the author ventured to point out that the fossil record of the **trilobites** which are among the first creatures to appear at the creation of life is complex in the Cambrian, but becomes simpler before they die out in the Silurian. Also he found a similar characteristic concerning the **graptolites**. The most complex type are the first, and they are the most simple just before they die out. When this book was revised by Dr Stubblefield, he completely omitted these doubts expressed by the original author, Dr Davies (page 134, *Who Was Adam?* E. K. Victor Pearce).

14. The **Primeval Soup Fraud.** Communist-Marxism was determined to spread atheism around the world and realised that they had to prove that life could accidentally arise from non-living matter. To do this they supported a theory that life could accidentally arise from a primordial soup in earth's early history. To propagate this to the western universities, they financed books by Professor Oparin whose western representative was Dr Haldane. This theory is no longer held in science, though there are some who still try to forget that. But scientists have analysed the actual characteristics of early earth and found that there was no such soup.

15 The first real scientist of Darwin's day to use proper scientific method was Gregor Mendel in the 1850s, but his findings on dominant and recessive genes were ignored because it was thought that they would demolish the evolution theory. Only in 1900 were his findings released to the public, when they thought it could be explained away. Darwin thought that what an animal developed in its lifetime could be passed on to its offspring. Mendel showed that only what

was in the DNA code could be inherited. Now, according to the Hardy–Weinberg equations there are 16 variants for any one gene, but they are inviolable and a recessive gene can appear again after many generations. It is this, which gives variations like those in dogs, not evolution.

7 SCIENTISTS TURN TO FAITH

Some of the leading scientists who have worked out the operation of the various parts of the cell are Christians. I mentioned, for example, Professor Kreb of Oxford who was responsible for working out the operation of the mitochondrion power station which is given the scientific name of Kreb's cycle. This power station supplies fuel for all the machinery of the cell in a similar way that a car needs fuel to work its engine. Professor Kreb adds significantly that the whole power station needs the fuel which it produces to start up its own machinery to produce the fuel which it uses. He implies that there must have been a Creator who completed the whole process and provided the fuel in the first place.

When we look into the personnel responsible for much of life's researches, we find that a high percentage of them are Christians. How is it, then, that the media gives the impression very often that science is against religion? Not everybody understands that there was a major propaganda organisation to promote atheism, funded by the Soviet Union. Let me quote Dr Jim Brookes, who was vice-president of the Geological Society. He says,

> The Soviet Union, under the initial lead of Academician Professor Alexsandr Oparin, were pioneers in studies on the origin of life to further the influence of Marxist–Leninist doctrine. British scientific colleagues and supporters, Professor J.B.H. Haldane (biophysicist) and Professor J.D. Bernal (crystallographer), were both opposed to religious beliefs . . . these studies deliberately aimed to focus scientific thinking away from religion.

It is therefore relevant for me to tell you that I attended the last lecture of Professor Haldane. He said that he wanted to say that he now felt the need for religion but that he didn't want to tell his friends because they would think he had let them down. In a similar way, Dr Julian Huxley, the son of the great propagandist of Darwin, wrote a book near the end of his career, speaking of his need for religion, as he called it. It is surprising how many eventually turn to God from their former unbelief. It does seem that God has implanted in us a kind of subconscious spiritual need. I was phoned by a professor from the biological department of University College London. He said that he had been an aggressive atheist for 40 years but having read my book *Who Was Adam?* he had become a believer. He invited me for tea to discuss various issues. I gladly accepted his invitation and he revealed that he was now greatly concerned for his son, whom he had brought up as an aggressive atheist and needed prayer and advice on how to bring the truth to him.

CHECKPOINTS

FURTHER QUOTES

1. Another scholar, Dr L.R. Croft, who is a lecturer in Biological Sciences at Salford University, has called Oparin's theory 'The Great Scientific Soup Myth'. He is referring to earth's early history, not to the early universe, as I have said, so do not get confused. Dr Croft says that life could not arise by accident and adds 'I am astonished that Oparin, a dedicated Marxist, could have succeeded in converting most of Western society to his belief in the so-called "primeval soup" ' (*How Life Began*, Evangelical Press, 1988, p 113). 'It is true to say,' says Dr Croft, 'that no other apostle of Marx has been so successful in the promulgation of his gospel of materialism . . . It comes as no surprise to find that Oparin was awarded the greatest honour of the Soviet Union.' The Soviet Union financed Oparin's books to make them cheap for universities around the world.

2. The physicist, Freeman Dyson, remarked in 1985, 'The Oparin picture . . . was popular, not because there was any evidence to support it, but because it seemed to be the only alternative to Biblical creation.' 'This view,' says Croft, 'was echoed by Sir Fred Hoyle. It is remarkable that over the past half century, the scientific world had almost, without exception, believed a theory for which there is not a single supporting fact.'

3. Dr Francis Crick, who discovered the structure of the DNA code, was originally an atheist, but in his book reporting the remarkable structure, he quotes at the beginning of the chapter, the statement of Salvador Dali: 'For me this is the real proof of the existence of God.' Notice that he does not make this his own quotation; perhaps he had not reached that state where he could be bold enough to do so, but he quotes another one who does it for him. Again, when he describes the

operation of the ribosomes which interpret the instructions and speaks of the mechanics necessary to operate them, he says that they have over 200 different operations, each enzyme with its own special key, to start his ribosome and they are also assisted by assistant mechanics and they must all operate together. For this, he says, there would be 'needed 200 frozen miracles'. Fancy an atheist asking for 200 frozen miracles!

4. Take another couple of scientists who set out on their career to explain all life as a result of accidents chosen by environment: Professor Fred Hoyle and Dr Wickramasinghe. They explain that as students they were brainwashed to explain everything without God, but now 'we realise that the only logical way to life is creation – and not accidental random shuffling. I am 100 per cent certain that life could not have started spontaneously on Earth,' says Wickramasinghe, who has worked with Hoyle since 1962. Other top ranking scientists have reached similar conclusions.

5. Here is a list of some of the modern research scientists who find that the evidence is for a creator. They are all leaders in their own field.

The Field of Astrophysics
Professor George Gamov
Dr Le Matre
Professor Fred. Hoyle
Dr R Wickramasinghe
Sir Bernard Llovell (and 40 others at Jodrell Bank).

The Field of Molecular Biology
Professor Malcolm Dixon (Head of Cambridge Enzyme-Biology Dept.)
Professor Kreb (Oxford Micro-Biology Dept.)
Dr L.C. Croft (Salford University 'How Life Began')
Sir Alistair Hardy (Oxford)
'21 Scientists who tell their own stories' in Dr Eric Barnett's book

Dr Jim Brooks, Vice-Pres. Geological Society.

Illuminating Quotations

Dr F. Crick, Nobel Prize winner (DNA structure) quotes Salvador Dali:

'The announcement of Watson & Crick on the DNA Code is for me the real proof of the EXISTENCE OF GOD!'

Dr F Crick also asks for: 'Two hundred frozen miracles' to explain the existence of 200 robot enzymes in the cell to start the machinery of special ribosome production units.

DARWIN'S CONVERSION CONFIRMED

Those who denied that Darwin was converted made several wrong assumptions:

i.   That he was converted on his deathbed in the spring
ii. That it was through Lady Hope who visited him
iii. That James Fegan only gave temperance lectures.

ANSWER

1. He was converted over a year earlier, not by Lady Hope but by the evangelist James Fegan who had been invited by Darwin to preach in his village. The present curator, Nina Strachey, confirmed this in 1999 in her letter to Miss Ward in which she quotes Darwin's letter of thanks to Fegan:

> Your services have done more in the village in a few months than all our efforts for many years. We have never been able to reclaim a drunkard, but through your services I do not know that there is a single drunkard left in the village.

2. The curator claims however that they were only temperance meetings, but the evangelist himself wrote:

> The services I held were attended sometimes by members of the Darwin Family and regularly by members of their household . . . at the services Parslow, the old family butler was converted to God . . . also Mrs Sales and others.

Alfred Tiffin in 'An Account of the Life and Work of J.W.C.

Fegan wrote: 'His passion was to win souls and to preach salvation.' Wherever a humanitarian mission took him 'he would preach the gospel with persuasive power'. 'The winning of souls he knew to be above all other considerations.'
This makes it clear they were **gospel** temperance meetings, as does a report in the *Christian Herald* of 21st December 1881.

3. Lady Hope only visited Darwin later, after his conversion, and six months **before** his death, to confirm the good news and was then invited to preach in his summer house about 'Jesus Christ and his salvation'. His wife in her letters reveals that they were having powerful prayer meetings in their house, and most of their servants were converted, especially Darwin's butler and personal friend. A former curator, Sir Hedley Atkins, said that one objector was 'wrong in her published statement' . . . perhaps she was carried away by her indignation!

8 DARWIN'S SECOND THOUGHTS

The other objection we must deal with is that Darwin 'never recanted any of his scientific views'. However, the following report was published in the *Bromley and Kentish Times* with the recollections of a Mr A.H. Nicholls who was closely acquainted with the servants of Darwin's household who had nursed him through his final illness:

> . . . this lady who had been in attendance on Darwin prior to his death had informed him that he requested her to read the New Testament to him and asked her to arrange for the Sunday School children to sing, 'There is a green hill far away'. This was done and Darwin, who was greatly moved, said, 'How I wish I had not expressed my theory of evolution as I have done.'

It is probable that the 'lady who nursed Darwin', was Mrs Evans. She had been with the Darwin household as a nurse for many years and as she was a member of the Gospel Hall congregation, she could have easily arranged for the Sunday School to sing an Easter hymn for Darwin.

CHECKPOINTS

DARWIN'S CONVERSION

1. Darwin's conversion reported by Lady Hope. Who was she?
   (a) Daughter of General Sir Arthur Cotton
   (b) Wife of Admiral Sir James Hope
   (c) Author of 37 books (British Library)
   (d) Temperance worker

    (e)   converted by J. Fegan one year before death

2. Also reported by:
    (a)   James Fegan, evangelist, temperance advocate
    (b)   Ishmael Jones in *Christian Herald* periodical
    (c)   Booth Tucker of Salvation Army
    (d)   A.N. Nichols who also heard Darwin's regrets about evolution

3. Mission conversions on Darwin's lawn reported by:
    (a)   Darwin's wife Emma
    (b)   Darwin's butler
    (c)   *Bromley and Kentish Times*

4. Accuracy confirmed by:
    (a)   Sir H. Atkins, President of Royal College of Surgeons
    (b)   Darwin's reference to harmonium and summer-house meetings
    (c)   Darwin's letter to evangelist Mr J. Fegan
    (d)   Dr L.R. Croft of Salford University

5. Darwin:
    (a)   Regretted the results of his theory
    (b)   Regretted use made by Karl Marx, etc.
    (c)   Regretted use made by Haeckel
    (d)   Admitted in his book *Origin of Species* that fossil record looked like special creation
    (e)   Made regular donations to South American Missionary Society

9 GOD'S TIMING OF CREATION EVENTS

AN ASSESSMENT OF PREVAILING VIEWS

It is helpful to realise that there have been fashions of interpretation among Bible-believing scientists when it comes to relating Genesis and science. By Bible-believing scientists, I mean scientists who believe that the Bible is fully inspired by the Holy Spirit and therefore is true and accurate in all that it says. The term I shall use for such a person is 'Biblical scientist'.

EARTH DAYS OR GALAXY DAYS?

'And there was evening, and there was morning – the first day.'
'And there was evening, and there was morning – the second day'
(Gen 1:5,8, NIV).

It is important to understand that the correlation between the creation story and science is not dependent upon whether we regard these days as earth days of 24 hours or cosmic days of geological ages. The fact that the succession of events both physical and biological is similar, stands indisputable. The timing factor is a separate issue.

First we note that the days of creation do not commence until after the initial cosmic events, 'In the beginning'.

All the heavens, i.e. the universe in its earlier stages, were created before the days began to be recorded so that no time-scale can be assessed from the Genesis account, except that it was from the beginning onwards. This is followed by void and darkness of verse 2, into which many primeval processes can be fitted. The days following are then measured by the end of one day the beginning of the next. It is the end which marks the first day – a significance you should note.

In one of my books *Evidence for Truth – Science*, I give four or five interpretations accepted by various Christians, on how long creation took.

24-hour-day application
Thousand-year-day application
Age-day application
Creation revealed in six days' application
Modified Evolution Application

CHECKPOINTS

GOD'S TIMING AND HUMAN ASSUMPTIONS

The order of creation is more important than the length of time. Don't insist on voicing your pet time schedule!

Five fashions of Biblical scientists
1. Age-Day theory for creation days
In the 19th century most Biblical scientists accepted age-days. Founders of Creation Science Movement accepted this theory, as Dr David Rosevear said. Many in it now press for 24-hour days of creation. Founders and supporters of the age-day theory were Dr M. Davies, D. Dewar, Professor Ambrose Fleming, Professor F.A. Filby, Dr R.E.D. Clark, W. Beasley, Professor Rendle-Short.

2. 1000-year days then became popular
Adam lived nearly a thousand-year day (cf. Gen 2:17, RSV). According to Ussher, six millennial days have passed. Seventh millennial day of rest and Christ's reign is near (2 Pet 3:8).

3. **Revelation to Moses took six days**

   Advocated by Professor D. Wiseman, Assyriologist (London University).

   Accords with ancient Middle East methods.

   Professor Van der Spuy: similar 'six-day blueprint of billion-year programme'.

4. **Galaxy days 360 million years long**

   Galaxy takes 360 million years to revolve. Dust across the axis makes it go dark every revolution. 'It was dark. It was light, the second day' (light before the sun, Gen 1:8).

5. **24-hour days based on Exodus 20:11**

   A supporter, Professor Enoch says the sun was created *after* the earth. This misinterprets the Hebrew historic tense on fourth day. 'God *had* made the sun'. Difficult sixth day afternoon, when ten major events took place. Note that seventh day did not end (Gen 2:1–3). Hebrews 4 says God still rests.

Essentials: believe God's words to be true, but don't cause divisions over creation timing (1 Cor 13:2).

HOW LONG DID CREATION TAKE?

People often ask me which application is correct. Until now, I have said that it is my principle not to divulge the one I take, but that they should choose the one which they are happy with and not condemn someone else for a different opinion. I usually add that the important thing is that the order in Genesis chapter 1 is the same order which science has found in the universe. However I feel I should now give you my interpretation. The important question to ask is which application does the Bible support?

DOES MOSES GIVE A CLUE?

We have seen evidence that it was Moses who wrote Genesis chapters 1 and 2. Does he give an answer to this question? He also wrote Psalm 90 and in it he speaks about creation:

Psalm 90

1. 'Before the mountains were brought forth, or ever You had formed the earth and the world, even from everlasting to everlasting, you are God' (v 2, NKJV). It was natural that Moses who had written down what God had told him about creation, should comment upon it in his psalm, expressing his wonder at the glory of the eternal Creator.

2. 'For a thousand years in your sight are but as yesterday when it is passed, and as a watch in the night' (v 4). It is clear Moses is talking about creation. The formation of the mountains implies that while God was creating them the days were at least a thousand years long – likened to a watch in the night which was only an eighth of the Creator's day.

3. Verse 4: also refers to God making the earth long before that, assuming that would take even longer. The earth was made of dust, without shape (1:2), and according to recent investigation, dust was manufactured in the stars. They pressure-baked it into more complicated material.

4. All this would imply that when God made the earth, it took much longer than the length of time just to make the mountains: 'Before the mountains were brought forth or before even the earth and the world were made, even from everlasting to everlasting, You are God . . . For a thousand years in your sight are like yesterday when it is past, and like a watch in the night.'
   It is amazing to me that not too many people have noticed that **the writer of the account of creation has given us an application of the length of a creation day in his Psalm 90.**

5. Yom – Day. It has been claimed by some that the Hebrew word 'day' (*yom*) always means a 24-hour length. This is not supported by the authentic Hebrew concordances.

i) *Young's Analytical Concordance* lists 95 times when *yom* is used in the OT. In Moses' works, i.e. Genesis to Deuteronomy the term day is used 65 times, but 19 of these refer to a **period** of time not a 24-hour day.

ii) *Cruden's, Concordance of the Bible,* lists 3 meanings to the word *yom.* The third: 'Any period of action or state of being, without definite reference to time.' Several examples are given which usually have the meaning 'when' and 'sometimes is so translated'. Genesis 2:4 refers to all six days as one day, summing up the chapter of creation before it as, 'These are the generations of the heavens and the earth when they were created, in the day that the Lord God made the earth and the heavens.'

iii) *Bagster's Hebrew Concordance* agrees and shows a significant number of times that *yom* is used for a period of time.

iv) Safarti is not correct in saying the Hebrew *yom* always meant 24 hours.

v) The Hebrew *ereb* (evening) literally means 'conclusion' and *boker* (morning) means 'beginning'.

THE ORIGIN OF CREATION SCIENCE

It is admitted by the present 24-hour Day protagonists that the founders of Creation Science were mostly advocates of Day Periods of unspecified length for the days of Genesis. These founders named their organisation The Evolution Protest Movement. It was founded in 1932 by Sir Ambrose Fleming, a famous scientist. He was joined by other scientists who were Christians. That was the time I also joined. Much later, the chairman of the movement, D.T. Rosevear with his committee, renamed the organisation Creation Science Movement, which was better and a more positve title but unfortunately they adopted an exclusive Young Earth policy of 24-hour creation days.

In his explanation in the *Creation Journal*, the chairman admits that most of their founders were period-day advocates and he gives their names: Dr Merson Davies, D. Dewar, Professor

F.A. Filby, Dr R.E.D. Clark, Walter Beasley and Professor Rendle-Short. The astonishing news is that now the movement only propagates Young Earth theories. It does not allow on its platform anyone who believes that the days were long periods of time. Anyone who holds this opinion is rigorously condemned even though he is a creationist. This greatly harms the effectiveness of the movement and allows the entrance of some serious inaccuracies. My prayer is that they will return to the original policy. This will honour the founders and concentrate on the essentials of God's truth.

10 THE GARDEN OF EDEN DISCOVERED

Where did farming begin? Archaeology has traced the geographical centre right back to where the Bible says it was. At first they looked at other places thinking that farming started there – Europe, then Egypt, then Palestine, then the fertile crescent of the Middle East. If they had looked at where the Bible said it started, they would have saved a lot of wasted time.

You will find in Genesis 2:10–14 that Eden was in the headwaters of the four rivers, Pison, Gihon, Tigris and Euphrates. These rivers rise on the plateau heights of Eastern Turkey.

Some have different ideas about where it was. Some have said it was in Mesopotamia, or even in the delta of the Persian Gulf at the mouths of the Tigris and Euphrates rivers.

Don't be deceived by 'tourist ideas', or comments by amateurs

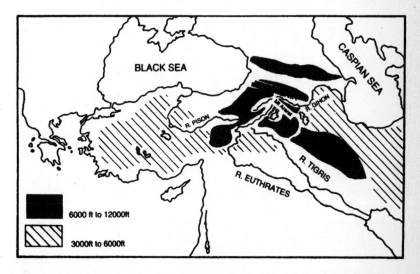

Fig.8. The headwaters of four rivers rising in the Ararat and Armenian mountain ranges.
This answers the description given in Genesis of the location from which farming began.

who have done no empirical research. There is a clear geographical location given in those verses in Genesis.

Flannery, in a symposium of world prehistoric archaeologists, draws attention to dry farming by the early farmers. At Ali Kosh 9,500 years ago, cereals were planted in such conditions. The small early dry farming village on the Kozistan steppe of south-west Iran, also produced 10,000 identifiable bones from 35 species of domesticated animals. A typical dry farming garden is shown below.

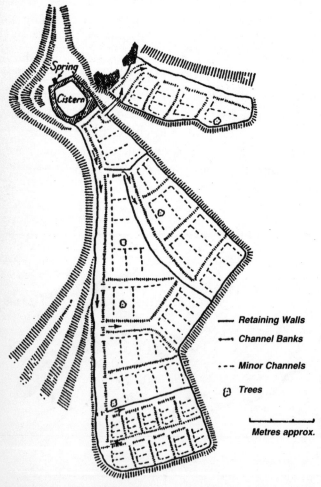

——— Retaining Walls

◄——◄ Channel Banks

- - - Minor Channels

⊕ Trees

Metres approx.

Fig. 9. Neolithic dry farming garden.
Rainless area irrigated by water seeping through rocks (Genesis 2:6) typical of dry farming methods in the Garden of Eden area and still used today in Arizona by Pueblo Indians.

Courtesy: C. Daryll Ford 'Habitat, Economy and Society' Methuen

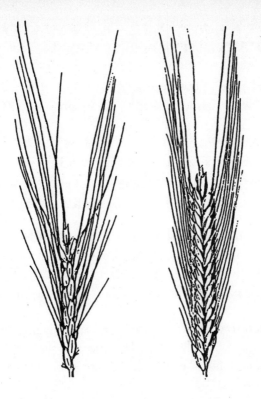

Fig.10. Wild grasses of the Middle East developed by man into cultivated wheats and barleys.
(left) The diploid wheat *Titicum boeoticum,* wild ancestor of Einkorn, the remains of which have been found in the Garden of Eden area; *(right) T. Monococcum,* cultivated Einkorn. Approx. nat. size. *After E. Schiemann.*

Courtesy Sonia Cole, The Neolithic Revolution, British Museum, 1959.

CHECKPOINTS

GARDEN OF EDEN

1. Where?

Source of four rivers, therefore highlands of western Turkey, not Mesopotamian valley. 'Eden' means plateau.

Lake Van: source of rivers Pison into Black Sea, Gihon into Caspian, Tigris and Euphrates into Persian Gulf.

Evidence: pollen core samples

Archaeological succession (pottery, etc.)
World Conference of Archaeologists.

When?
Archaeologist: 12,000 years ago
Bible tables: Ussher revised by Campion – 10,000 BC

2. **Origin of farming**
Where Bible says Adam started (Gen 2:8,15)
- Dry farming techniques – no rain. Gen 2:6. 'ed' = water not mist. cf. Pueblo-style dry farming or 'flood water farming'.
- Flint tools before metals of Genesis 4:22. Adam's tool kit.
- First domestication. God brought animals to Adam. Thirty-five species at Ali-Kosh.
- Cereals native to that area. Wheat, barley, legumes.

3. **Migration to world** (evidence: stone axes, digging sticks)
Europe: along Danube, and Mediterranean shores.
East: India, China Yellow River (reaping knives) to America (Bering Straits).
South: Sahara desert lush vegetation (before Flood), Africa.

4. **Tablets** Genesis 2:4 onwards is *not* a second creation account. Toledot tablet method (v 4) sums up before sequel is added. Higher critics did not know this, and still ignore archaeological evidence.
Two names for God on one tablet source was common usage 2,500 BC (Ebla tablets use Lord and God together, i.e. Yah and El).

11 ANTHROPOLOGY SUPPORTS THE BIBLE

The theories of anthropology have also been reversed, largely through Professor Evans-Pritchard's insistence on fieldwork.

Whereas before the 1930s, an evolutionary concept of religion was that it developed from animism and magic to polytheism and then finally to monotheism, fieldwork reversed this and anthropologists now realise that belief in one Creator God preceded all other religious concepts. This gradually corrupted to polytheism, and finally to the placating of an extensive array of nature spirits. Some popular lecturers in theology seem unaware of this change and continue to reshuffle the Old Testament documentary-wise, changing its story of one God revealing himself into an evolutionary process of man's groping from animism to monotheism. In this way many are being persuaded to forsake the claims of Scripture that God has uniquely revealed himself through the Torah and the prophets and finally through the Christ.

FIELDWORK EVIDENCE FOR PRIMITIVE BELIEF IN ONE GOD

These people believed in a High God Creator. These 'world views', as anthropologists call them, are quite abstract in their concepts. Dr Pospisil, living among the Kapauki in 1954 reported, 'This stone-age tribe was not without its abstract philosophy. God is omniscient, omnipotent, and omnipresent, credited with the creation of all things and with having determined all events.'

CHECKPOINTS

EVIDENCE FOR THE FALL

1. Wickedness gradually increases

First pioneers along Danube needed no fortifications.

Second Danubians fortified. Earth gods, suggestive figurines. First Stone-Age city had no such figurines (Gen 6:4) and no warfare.

Oral tradition from primitives of age of innocence, e.g. China Miao, Andamanese, New Guinea Kanpauki, Australian Aboriginal folklore, First American Indians. Universal original belief in Creator, 'Sky God', before polytheism and animism.

2. Sin-offerings commence

Abel's sacrifice (Gen 4:2–5).

- Increase in lamb bones in Shanidar-Zarzi complex, Karim Shahir, Bolt Cave, Jarmo, Ali Kosh.
- Worldwide primitive custom of propitiation.
  Professor Zwemer: e.g. Eskimos, Pygmies, Algonguins Bushmen, and Veddas.
  Professor Evans-Pritchard: Nuer tribe, Upper Nile, confession over ox sacrifice.
- Bible evidence. Tribes always degenerated from original revelation e.g.,
  Cain's descendants. Tower of Babel.
  Abraham's relatives. (Lot and Ammonites, Moabites) Jacob's descendants: Esau and Edomites, then Israel and Judah sacrificed children to demon gods.
  Then idolatry into the medieval church as prophesied.

Romans 1:28: 'Did not retain God in their knowledge and degenerated into immorality, wickedness, greed, murder, hatred of God' (translated from the Greek text).

Learn Romans 3:23; 5:12 and 5:8.

12 CREATION TEACHING AND THE FIVE BOOKS OF MOSES

WHERE DID CREATION TEACHING ORIGINATE?

The oldest book to teach it was the one written by Moses. It is now contained as the first five books of the Bible, Genesis, Exodus, Leviticus, Numbers and Deuteronomy, and was originally called The Book of the Law or the Torah. The Torah was divided into five in 285 BC for the Greek translation and now is also known as the Pentateuch.

In it Moses claims that God the Creator revealed himself to him, so it will be relevant to look at these claims. The reason for our need to do so is because about 150 years ago many who did not believe in creation claimed that Moses did not write his work fourteen centuries before Christ, but that the Torah was a package of religious ideas which had evolved down the thousand years since Moses and that they had been collected and not put into a book until a thousand years later in about 400 years BC.

The reasoning behind this was that they thought **religion had also evolved**, and that it was not revealed by God to Moses as claimed. It was thought that Levitical religion described by Moses fourteen centuries BC was not developed until four centuries BC.

It tells us of creation, man's rebellion against God, the Flood, God's choice of a nation through which the Saviour of mankind would come, the deliverance of that nation from slavery, the giving of God's Laws and the way of atonement. From the first synagogues even to today, the Torah is kept in scroll form in a beautifully made cabinet in the holiest place of the synagogue which is called the Ark.

EVIDENCE THAT MOSES WAS THE AUTHOR OF GENESIS TO DEUTERONOMY

We must remember that Moses lived in the greatest period of Israelite history. He it was who led Israel out of the slavery of Egypt. It would have been strange if he had made no record of such events, especially as every monument of Egypt in his time depicted scribes recording every event, even routine daily agricultural processes. That Moses also had the habit of recording current history is seen in Deuteronomy 31:22, 'Moses wrote this song the same day'. Other references to Moses' writing is in Exodus 17:8–14; 24:4,7; 34:4; Deuteronomy 31:9–12, 24–26. Moreover, Numbers 33:2 tells us that Moses methodically recorded all the travels of his 40 years' leadership.

That a regular account was kept seems to be the point of the remark in Exodus 17:14, 'Write this for a memorial in The Book' as though there was a regular account kept in a well-known book.

COURSE MATERIAL IN ERROR

Experts have since found that the literary methods evident in the Pentateuch are those of the time of Moses and not of a later date when methods changed. Experts in this practical field are Professor Kenneth Kitchen, professor of Archaeology and Oriental Studies; Dr D. Wiseman, professor of Assyriology and a Semitist; and Professor Alan Millard. All have recognised international standing.

Professor Kitchen himself has translated tablets and scripts from treaties in Hittite, Elamite, Sumerian, Aramaic languages as well as Egyptian, Ugaritic, Akkadian, etc.

In a typical course for Lay Readers in one diocese there was no mention of their scholarly, factual findings, and so I have been asked to supply this lack. Neither was any mention made of up-to-date scholars who have taught in theological colleges such as J.A. Motyer; Dr John Wenham; Dr W.J. Martin; Donald Robinson; Professor F.F. Bruce; A. Gibson; Bishop John Robinson; R.T. France and others.

These experts found that ancient tablets and scripts used both Divine names in their accounts, sometimes together and sometimes singly according to the subject material. They did not indicate different authorship or sources.

The old-fashioned Higher Critics did not know this, so they divided up the Bible stories according to the name used for God. By doing this, they made the one version into two or three, and by doing so they artificially created contradictory versions.

To read more on these tablets, including the exciting discoveries of the Ebla Tablets, see Chapter 15.

CHECKPOINTS

QUESTIONS ABOUT THE AUTHORSHIP OF MOSES

First, do the first five books of the Bible really claim Moses as the author? Second, was a developed religion practised as early as Moses? Third, do the writing methods of the ancients justify the dividing up of Moses' work into later documents, called the Documentary Theory?

1. Do Moses' writings claim his authorship?

At the end of his book we read the words 'When Moses had finished writing the words of this law in a book to the very end, Moses commanded the Levites who carried the Ark of the Covenant of the Lord "Take this Book of the Law (Torah) and put it by the side of the Ark of the Covenant of the Lord your God, that it may be there for a witness against you" ' (Deut 31:24–26).

What was this book? Was it the whole of the works from Genesis to Deuteronomy, or Deuteronomy only, which is what some thought? In thinking this they did not know the history of how in 285 BC the works of Moses were divided up into the five books that we have today by the Greeks who wanted the whole works of Moses translated into their own language. Evidence of this can be seen when one reads the end of one book and continues into the beginning of the next – they continue from each other as if it was originally an unbroken work. For example, the end of Numbers speaks of the commandments and ordinances, which the Lord gave to Moses in the Plains of Moab and continues on into Deuteronomy, speaking about the journey in the land of Moab.

Consider: Have we any statements in that work that Moses wrote down what God told him? That God often spoke audibly to him and that he wrote down what he said verbatim?

The answer is yes; about eight times we get such statements.

a) 'The Lord called Moses, and spoke to him from the tent of meeting, saying "Speak to the people of Israel, and say to them, when any man of you brings an offering to the Lord, you shall bring your offering of cattle from the herd or from the flock" ' (Lev 1:1). Throughout this book the words are represented as dictated to Moses and recorded by him.

b) In the book of Exodus the phrase is frequently repeated 'then the Lord said to Moses . . .' (see Ex 17:14).

c) A reference to the actual writing and completion of a book is also in Deuteronomy 18, where God says that when you have a king, the king 'shall write for himself in a book a copy of this law [Torah], from that which is in charge of the Levitical priests'.

2. The next question is, does Moses claim that God spoke to him audibly, in a way that he did not speak to any other person?

The answer is in Numbers 12. It arose out of the jealousy of Miriam and Aaron against Moses and God suddenly intervened as spokesman for Moses. Miriam and Aaron asked,

'Has the Lord indeed spoken only through Moses? Has he not spoken through us also?' Then suddenly the Lord said to Moses and Aaron and Miriam, 'Come out you three! Go to the Tent of Meeting.' And the three of them came out and the Lord came down in a pillar of cloud and stood at the door of the tent and called Aaron and Miriam and they both came forward. Then God said to them, 'Hear my words! If there is a prophet among you, I the Lord make myself known to him in a vision. I speak with him in a dream. But not so with my servant Moses. He is entrusted with all my house. With him I speak mouth to mouth clearly and not in dark speech and he beholds the form of the Lord. Why then were you not afraid to speak against my servant Moses?' And the anger of the Lord was against them. And he departed.

3. Has archaeology also given support to the Mosaic authorship of the Torah or five books of Moses?

a. Professor Kenneth Kitchen and others reveal that the Torah is written on the legal code system of the Hittites, in which all the ritual is enacted from Exodus to Deuteronomy. It was the legal system of the time and a covenant between people had to be stated, written out and summarised as in the commandments and in the Ten Commandments, and then sealed by the blood of sacrifice sprinkled upon the Book of the Covenant, and this is referred to . . .

b. Also, the people had to swear solemnly that they would keep the covenant or suffer the consequences. Then there had to be stated a series of curses upon the people who broke the agreement, followed by a series of blessings upon those who kept the agreement (see Leviticus); read out publicly every year (in Deuteronomy), with the curses and the blessings. This legal system was the one operative in Moses' time and not since.

c. 'Much information on covenants and treaties in the Near East has come to light. From no less than 45 treaties from the archives of the Hittites, Ugarit, etc., it has been possible to establish the clear pattern.'

CHECKPOINTS

UNDERSTANDING THE STYLE

Genesis to Deuteronomy is a covenant style on the legal require-
ments of Moses' time fourteen centuries BC. It must state:

1. The author of the Covenant (Jehovah).
2. Reference to earlier relations (Patriarchs in Genesis).
3. Basic stipulations (Ten Commandments) followed by more
   details (Ex 21 to Num 10).
4. Arrangement for deposit of the Covenant in the vassal's sanctuary (recorded only in Deut 31:24–25).
5. Periodic reading of the Covenant terms to the people (recorded only in Deuteronomy 31:11).
6. Witnesses (Ex 24:7 & 8) sealed by sprinkling the blood of the
   Covenant.
7. Curses for disobedience to the Covenant and blessing for
   keeping it (Lev 26 and Deut 27–30).
8. Oath of obedience with solemn ceremony (Ex 19:8).

This is also fully documented by V. Korosec of Leipzig and G.E.
Mendenhall (Oxford Ashmoleum Museum).

CHECKPOINTS

MOSES IN A TIME MACHINE

In an imaginary six-day space–time journey, we see how God created the universe and man, male and female. If space and time are relative, it avoids conceptual difficulties; so we speed back in time with NASA probe to see God actually creating the universe and how it all accords with Genesis and we converse with Moses as he writes it down! (Set out in author's *Evidence for Truth: Science.*)

The sixth day has the longest programme
In it Moses sets down the blueprint for the following busy schedule:

1. God made the land animals from the ground.
2. God created Adam from the dust and nuclear acids left by supernovae.
3. God planted the garden of Eden and made trees and plants to grow.
4. God placed Adam in the garden to cultivate it.
5. God told Adam not to eat the forbidden fruit.
6. God brought all the animals and birds to Adam to be named.
7. God put Adam into a deep sleep and removed a rib.
8. From a cell in his rib, by genetic engineering, he built the cell into a woman.
9. God introduced Adam to her who exclaims, 'At long last, one made flesh from my flesh!' (cells from my cells).
10. They were joined as husband and wife and became 'one flesh'.
11. God told Adam and Eve to populate the earth and subdue it.

It is exciting to watch the operations with the knowledge we now have of the seven enzymes for genetic engineering.

*Why not send for my audio-cassette from UCB, Hanchurch Christian Centre, Stoke-on-Trent, ST4.

CAIN'S WIFE

'Cain lay with his wife and she conceived and bare Enoch' (Gen 4:17). 'After Seth was born [when Adam was 130 years old], Adam lived 800 years and had other sons and daughters' (Gen 5:4).

As the reference comes after the statement that Cain had migrated eastwards, some have asked where did Cain find a wife? Cain's wife could have been one of his sisters – for Adam and Eve had daughters as well as sons (Gen 5:4) one of whom he may have married before he became a fugitive. Cain feared others when he said, 'I shall be a fugitive and wanderer in the earth and whosoever finds me will kill me.' Who would these other men be? By the time Adam and Eve were 130 years old (Gen 5:3), they would have lived long enough for their children's descendants to have increased to a population as large as 3,000,000 and to have travelled some distance.

We should not suppose that Çatal Hüyük is the actual city Cain built, for, as we have seen, when Cain fled from his homeland, he is said to have travelled 'eastward from Eden' (Gen 4:16 RSV) and dwelt in the land of Nod.

But the discovery of Çatal Hüyük does give us sound archaeological evidence that the Bible was right and that Cain and his contemporaries were capable of building cities in the New Stone Age.

CHECKPOINTS

CAIN'S CITY

1. **New Stone Age City** Genesis 4:17 was before metals in 4:22. Çatal Hüyük on Turkish Plateau discovered by Professor J. Mellaart.
   Before this discovery, some thought the Bible was wrong to speak of cities before the Bronze Age, because a city needed specialised trades to support it, and organisation.

2. **Çatal Hüyük, 8,000 population**, had trades, and market gardening outside the city.
   Traded volcanic glass tools for miles around, carpentry with flint tools.
   Weaving and dye-stamped cloth. Frescoes showed women in long dresses, and men in loin-cloth or skirt down to knees. Leopard-skin caps.

3. **Levels three and four** (five generations after Cain) Pictures of *pipes and harps* (Gen 4:17–21).
   Copper–Stone Age arrives, but not smelting.
   'Tubal-Cain was a *hammerer* of copper and iron' (Gen 4:22). Hebrew means hammerer. Smelting of iron came later, not until 1500 BC.

4. **Technological background** to Bible 10,000 to 1,500 BC is remarkable.
   New Stone Age, Copper–Stone Age, Bronze Age, Iron Age. Succession all correct.

5. **Population explosion** as in Genesis 6. Other city mounds in sight.
   In 130 years (Gen 5:3) computer estimates population at 3 million. By the time Cain built his stone-age city like Hüyük it would be populous.

6. **Religion. Hüyük** was very religious, but astray from truth One in three rooms were shrines to mother goddess .
Cain had refused lamb atonement (Gen 4:5; Heb 11:4).

13 FRESH EVIDENCE FOR THE FLOOD

In September 2000, new discoveries in the Black Sea convinced newspapers that the Bible Flood actually happened. Robert Ballard (the man who discovered the *Titanic*) funded by the National Geographic Society, found that the Black Sea was suddenly invaded by sea waters at the time of the biblical Flood. Before that there were fresh-water molluscs in the sea because it was blocked off from the Mediterranean, but after the Flood a salt-water species came. This also confirmed the discovery by the geologists Ryan and Pitman that the Flood had burst through the natural dam separating the Black Sea from the Mediterranean. Now a further surprise was revealed by Ballard; he had brought his expert instruments to bear upon the Black Sea. A remote-controlled submarine had discovered an ancient Neolithic village 300 feet below water on the north coast of the Black Sea. The inhabitants had been annihilated by that sudden invasion of ocean waters. The wood from which their huts had been made had been planed into planks and the catastrophe had happened at the beginning of the Copper–Bronze Age.

This is an amazing confirmation of the accuracy of Genesis. Chapter 4:22 tells us that the early Copper–Bronze Age only started just before the Flood (see chapter 10 of my book *Science*, concerning the cultural succession which archaeologists have found, showing that the Garden of Eden was in the Neolithic Age and was followed by the Copper–Bronze Age and then by Noah's Flood). This Neolithic site is 'close to the mouth of a river'. That is significant for that is the River Pison which the Bible says flows north from the Garden of Eden which is in the east centre of Turkey.

The Times leader of 14th September 2000 said, 'This week's findings are the first to prove that human beings were drowned or displaced by this flood.'

The Bible represents the Flood as coming mainly from the deep oceans. 'All the fountains of the great deep burst open' (Genesis 7:11). There was a good report in the *Daily Mail* but it made the common mistake of saying that the Flood lasted only 40 days. The Bible says it lasted one year and ten days. The 40 days' rain were only a prelude to the Flood which then lasted one year and ten days. The date of the start is given in Genesis 7:11. It was in Noah's 600th year, 2nd month and 17th day. It ended a year later on Noah's 601st year in the 2nd month on the 27th day (8:13 & 14). The flood waters had taken five months to reach their greatest height (7:24) – which covered Mount Ararat which is 16,000 feet high – and they took nearly eight months to drain away. The Bible indicates that the oceans and the waters under the earth had been flung out of their beds by a change of axis. The oceans would rush over the continents.

The comparatively new science of Palaeomagnetism shows that the earth has turned on a different pole in earlier times – probably where the magnetic pole is now. The geographic pole is now about 16 degrees away from the magnetic pole.

The deep oceans would have rushed over the continents, swept animals into caves, and even up mountains, to beat their bones into broken pieces.

CHECKPOINTS

WHERE DO DINOSAURS, FOSSILS & THE FLOOD COME IN TO GENESIS?

- Creation of the universe – the heavens – (Gen 1:1)
- Light in the universe before the sun (1:3)
- Formation of the earth
- Creation of **plant** life to put oxygen into the air (1:11)
- Fossils of **marine** life:
  1st – Swarms of small creatures (1:20)
  2nd – Great water monster (Hebrew – *taninim*) including dinosaurs (see 1:21)
  3rd – Flying insects (1:22)
- Creation of **land** animals (1:24):
  Fossils of dinosaurs *disappear* before mammals and humans appear
  Fossils of **mammals** (1:25)
  Fossils of **mankind** – male and female (1:27)
- **Flood** and Noah (Gen 6–8)
- Repopulation of earth
- Divided into languages at Tower of Babel. When? In the days of Peleg (Gen 10:25). Peleg was *five generations after Noah* (Gen 11:10–17) 'after the flood' (v 10).
- Three dispersions according to the Royal Anthropological Institute racial genetic samples.

This order in Genesis is the same as that discovered by scientists.

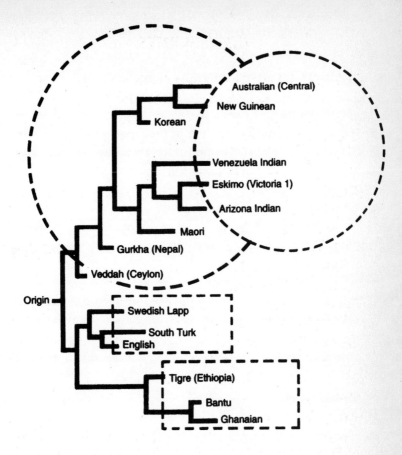

Fig. 11. Racial family tree computed from blood group gene frequencies
From Cavalli-Sforza and Edwards 1963. It demonstrates one origin of all races and separates clearly:
1. the three African groups from
2. the three European groups with
3. Asiatic, American Indian and Oceanic representatives occupying the other end of the tree and forming a more heterogeneous group.
Notice the three main overall groupings. These could be from Noah's sons.

According to Genesis, where does the *Flood fit in* with the order of events?

This is an important question as some seem to have been getting confused. The first chapter gives us the order of creation, the second chapter is the next instalment and begins by telling us about Adam and Eve and the Garden of Eden. It is after this that the story of the Flood begins to open up.

CHECKPOINTS

THE ORDER OF UNIVERSAL EVENTS

1. **The order of the fossils in the rocks is accounted for in Genesis 1 and not in the story of the Flood which came later in Genesis 6 to 9.** This demonstrates that it was not the Flood which laid down the fossils as some have suggested.

2. **The main source of the deluge was from 'the fountains of the great deep'.** So although there were 40 days' torrential rain, the water from the sky was not the chief source of the floodwaters.

3. **It was after the waters from the deep invaded the earth that they began to rise for 5 months until they were above the mountains,** and then it took another 7 months for them to return to their place. Recently it has been discovered and reported in science journals that there is more water under the earth than in the seas.

4. **The Bible tells us that the chief source of the Flood was from *below not above*.** 'On that day all the fountains of the **great deep** burst forth' (Gen 7:11).

5. **The Flood lasted for over a year** because the starting date given is the 600th year of Noah's life, in the second month on the seventeenth day (Gen 7:11); and then the date that it ended is 'the six hundred and first year . . . in the second month on the twenty-seventh day of the month, the earth was dry. And God said to Noah "Go out of the ark" ' (Gen 8:13–14).

6. **Note the tremendous volume of water** (it took 5 months for the Flood to reach its greatest height, 'At the end of 150 days the water ceased to rise. And in the seventh month of the Flood on the 17th day of the month the ark came to rest upon the mountains of Ararat' (Gen 8:3,4).

7. **What caused the oceans to flood out of their beds?** It was
   probably due to a change in the earth's axis. For evidence of
   this see Chapters 12 to 13 of my book *Evidence for Truth –
   Science* (Guildford: Eagle Books).

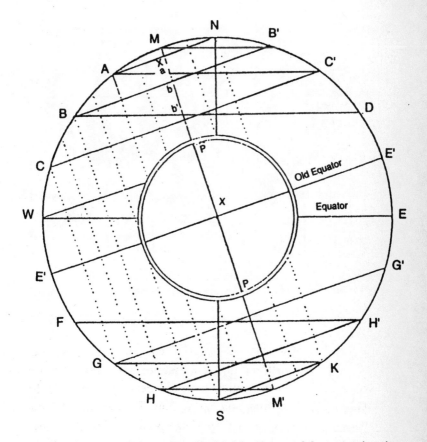

**Fig. 12. Diagram to illustrate the effects of the change of the magnetic axis
in causing the submersion of certain lands.**
Let the large circle represent a section of the earth; the interior small circle a sec-
tion of the earth's nucleus, in continuance.
NS and WE, the present axis and equator, marking the four points, North, South,
West and East.
M the magnetic north pole, 18½° N; and MM¹ the former poles and axis of both
the earth and nucleus before the deluge.
A, B and C, points on the earth's surface; A, 18½° distant from M; and B and
C at the same distance each from the other, on the same meridian arc.
AN, BB¹, CC¹, equidistant parallels of latitude upon the old axis; MB¹, AC¹ and
BD¹, equidistant parallels of latitude on the new axis and post-diluvian globe.

E¹E¹ the old equator, before the deluge.
GG¹, HH¹ and SK parallels of latitude on the old axis; FH¹, GK and HM¹, par-
allels of latitude on the new axis and present earth.
X the common centre; P and P the poles of the nucleus.
The dotted lines indicate the original polar parallelism acquired in the deposit of
the strata, now changed to oblique.

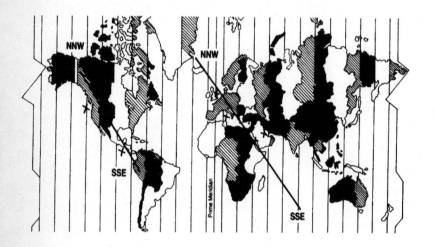

Fig. 13. Inclination of natural features to the existing axis of earth rotation.

CHECKPOINTS

CLUES TO THE CAUSE OF THE FLOOD

1. **Flood caused by a change of axis**
   Palaeomagnetism of rocks indicates it.
   Magnetic poles caused by independent inner core revolution.
   Outer crust geographical pole was once aligned with the core.
   Sudden realignment caused a huge surge of seawater sufficient
   to cover the land for a time.

2. **Effect of change of axis would be a worldwide flood**
   Water stationary on old poles would have to speed up to 300
   mph.

Oceans at old equator would swirl at an angle to new equator.
Oceans are 3 times as deep as the mountains are high.
Oceans cover over twice as much of globe as land.
Oceans would swirl out of the deep as in:
  'Fountains of the great deep burst out' (Gen 7:11).
  'The waters [from the deep] stood above the mountains
  . . . They might not again cover the earth' (Ps 104:6–9,
  RSV).
  Sun rose in new place 'to shake the wicked out of their new
  earth' (Job 38:12–15).
  Flood from around continents (2 Pet 3:5,6).
  Jesus said it '*Swept* them away' (Mt 24:39).
God tells Job the earth is like a cylinder seal which turns on a
spindle.

3. **Evidence of axis change**
New sea levels throughout the world. Fossil beaches.
Oceans were higher at old equator – centrifugal bulge. Fossil
beach through Andes 12,000 feet high.
Coral beds at an angle.
Mountain ranges at an angle.
Palaeomagnetism indicates big change in 'recent' human his-
tory.
Nations testify to a different pole star, i.e. Anaxagorus and St
Peter (2 Pet 3:6,7).

THE FLOOD BEYOND DOUBT

As André Parrot, the famous French archaeologist, points out, it
is difficult to doubt that such detailed and persistent records have
a factual basis. 'There can be no question that the Flood marked
a clear break in history,' he writes. 'The memory of it remained
vividly in men's minds as well in Mesopotamia as in Palestine.'
And again, 'The cataclysm was accompanied by destruction on
such a scale, and made such an impression, that it became one of
the themes of cuneiform literature.'

Genesis: the original version

There is, in the Babylonian tablets, little conception of God's grief at the sin and violence of mankind as in Genesis 6:5–14. These are the type of details which would be unpopular and get left out of later tablets.

> The LORD saw that the wickedness of man was great in the earth, and that every imagination of the thoughts of his heart was only evil continually. And the LORD was sorry that he had made man on the earth, and it grieved him to his heart. So the LORD said, 'I will blot out man whom I have created from the face of the ground, man and beast and creeping things and birds of the air, for I am sorry that I have made them.' But Noah found favour in the eyes of the LORD.
>
> These are the generations of Noah. Noah was a righteous man, blameless in his generation; Noah walked with God. And Noah had three sons, Shem, Ham, and Japheth.
>
> Now the earth was corrupt in God's sight, and the earth was filled with violence. And God saw the earth, and behold, it was corrupt; for all flesh had corrupted their way upon the earth. (RSV)

MYSTERY OF THE MAMMOTHS

The torrential volumes of ocean rushing over the heights would sweep along those huge whales, mammoths, rhinoceroses, hippopotamuses, all to be dashed into pieces. Fragments of teeth and fractured jaws and bits of skull of animals and man mixed up with the teeth of a lion or hyena have been found embedded in the hard breccia of caves. Here would be a massive elephant's tusk and there would be bits of horns and bones of dismembered beasts.

These all help us to imagine the tremendous sudden nature of the worldwide catastrophe and the great force and violence of the invasion of the continents. Near the North Pole, great mammoths would be engulfed in freezing seas and quickly frozen solid in blocks of ice.

Scores of these have been found when the melting ice in Siberia has disgorged a whole woolly elephant thousands of years old preserved fresh in the ice with the grass it was eating, when it was suddenly overtaken by the freezing sea, still green in its mouth (see Fig 14). An Oxford anthropologist told me he had attended a mammoth-steak dinner made from these deep frozen mammoths. He said the meat was delicious!

Fig. 14. Mammoth from Beresovka, Siberia. Note the attitude of the beast, as though endeavouring to extricate itself.

PRE-FLOOD ANIMALS IN AMERICA

In America, huge mammoths perished and horses, lions, tigers and other wild beasts and even camels were drowned right across the continent.

Flood Evidence Comes from:
America – Alabama, Fort Rock, Wildcat
Egypt – between the Gerzian and Amratian
England – Cambridgeshire
Europe – Danube Valley
Mesopotamia – Ten sites of cities in Genesis 10
Australia – Timor Sea
Black Sea – from fresh to salt water
    (Further details in *Evidence for Truth: Science*.)

CHECKPOINTS

WORLDWIDE EVIDENCE

1. **Skeletal**
   Animal bones on mountain tops. Not syncline fossils.
   Mammoths of Siberia frozen whole in ice blocks.
   Mammoth bones frequently uncovered in USA.
   Whales in Alabama (mid-continent) bones used for fences.
   Pre-Flood animals under stratum in USA (horses, lions etc).

2. **North and South American sites with Flood disjunction**
   Wildcat Cave (Dr D. Cole).
   'Dirty Shame' site.
   Fort Rock, Oregon.
   Lake Titicaca in Andes agricultural ridges now frozen at 12,000 feet.

3. **Calendar changes made after Flood**
   Greater angle made bigger seasonal contrasts (Gen 8:22).
   Only 360 days in year before Flood.
   Reason for 360 degrees in circle and compass.

   Ancient calendars had 360 days and 12 months of 30, e.g.:
   Noah's calendar, 5 months = 150 days to Flood peak (Gen 7:11; 8:3,4).
   Hindu calendar, 360 with 12 x 30 (Thibant's *Astronomie*).
   Chinese calendar, 360 with 12 x 30 (per Medhurst).
   Greek calendar, the same (per Herodotus).
   Babylon cuneiform script had 360. Same for Romans (Plutarch) and Incas of Peru and Mayas, Persia and Egypt (total 10 nations).
   Proves planetary disturbance.

CHECKPOINTS

THE CHRONOLOGY OF THE FLOOD

There were 40 days during which the rain fell (Gen 7:12)   40 days

Throughout another 110 days the waters continued to rise, making 150 days in all for their 'prevailing' (Gen 7:24)   110 days

The waters occupied 74 days in their 'going and decreasing' (AV margin). This was from the 17th of the seventh month to the 1st of the tenth month (Gen 8:5). There being 30 days to a month at that time, the figures in days are 13 plus 30 plus 1   74 days

Forty days elapsed before Noah sent out the raven (Gen 8:6,7)   40 days

Seven days elapsed before Noah sent out the dove for the first time (8:8). This period is necessary for reaching the total and is given by implication from the phrase 'other seven days' (Gen 8:10)   7 days

Seven days passed before sending out the dove for the second time (Gen 8:10)   7 days

Seven more days passed before the third sending of the dove (Gen 8:12)   7 days

Up to this point 285 days are accounted for, but the next episode is dated the 1st of the first month in the 601st year. From the date in Genesis 7:11 to this point in Genesis 8:13 is a period of 314 days; therefore an interval of 29 days elapses.   29 days

From the removal of the covering of the ark to the very end of the experience was a further 57 days.   57 days

TOTAL   371 days

With acknowledgment to the New Bible Commentary IVF.

14   SHARING A COMMON ANCESTRY

MIGRATION FROM ARARAT TO IRAQ AND BABEL

Now the whole world had one language and a common speech. As men moved eastward, they found a plain in Shinar and settled there' (Gen 11:1 NIV).

With the passing of years, the survivors of the Flood made their way along the Iranian mountain plateau south-eastwards. Some of them descended into the Indus valley towards the East, where their culture has been excavated at Harappi. Others descended westwards into the Mesopotamian valley. Here they are called Ubaidians, from their type site at al'Ubaid. In the totally different environment of Mesopotamia, they were forced to use new materials for the buildings and crafts.

The evidence supports the Bible by showing that the earth was repopulated from a common ancestry and from a common geographical area, from which we can trace the spread of mankind after the cultural hiatus of the Flood incident.

NIMROD THE MIGHTY HUNTER

The latest sports news of the day 3,500 BC makes a headline in Genesis 10:8. Featured large is the hero Nimrod – a name which has fascinated mankind ever since. He was one of those charismatic pioneers, not only of sport, but also in the founding and building of several city-states. This was after the devastation of the Flood. What a list of achievements he had to his name.

First, consider his sport. His name was proverbial. 'Nimrod, the mightly hunter before the Lord.' In addition, he planned and built separate autonomous communities. They became known as city-states. The planning was to avoid a centralised despotic empire. Each city-state would have the local interests of the community at heart. The ruins of each city are, today, the prime interest of archaeologists and anthropologists. Genesis 10:8–12 is a running commentary upon their discoveries:

> And Cush begat Nimrod: he began to be a mighty one in the earth. He was a mighty hunter before the LORD: wherefore it is said, Even as Nimrod the mighty hunter before the LORD. And the beginning of his kingdom was Babel, and Erech, and Accad, and Calneh, in the land of Shinar. Out of that land went forth Asshur, and builded Nineveh, and the city Rehoboth, and Calah, and Resen between Nineveh and Calah: the same is a great city. (AV)

These cities are now archaeological sites. The most famous is Babylon. This was called Babel at first. To my mind, the fact that things went wrong at Babylon centuries later is not the fault of Nimrod. Late in history, Babylon became all that is typical of false religion. Also ambitious despots forsook Nimrod's ideology of local government and created for the area an empire which was to impose its errors and rule all over the then-known world.

CHECKPOINTS

HOW ARCHAEOLOGY FITS IN WITH
GENESIS HISTORY

1. **Before the Flood:** Genesis 2:8–6:13
   Shanidar-Zarzi complex of caves, and earliest farming experiments 10,000 BC
   First City-building Era:
   New Stone Age and Chalcolithic Çatal Hüyük, Hacilar.
   Natufian and New Stone Age Jericho.
   North Mesopotamian villages of Hassuna and Halaf type.

2. **The Flood:** Genesis 6:14–9:17
   Post diluvian dispersion, Genesis 9:18–10:32.

3. **After the Flood**
   Commencement of Second City-building Era in South Mesopotamia:
   * Genesis 11:2
     Migration from Ararat along Iranian plateau (Zagros Mountains) south-eastwards, then descent from the east on to the flood-plain of Sumer (Shinar) of South Mesopotamia.
     Ubaidian colonisation of the marshes (c.3900 BC); reed huts, irrigation; an important step forward. Some hundreds of years represented by the word 'settled' (RSV).
   * Genesis 11:3
     Mud bricks appear first in the Ubaidian phase as there was no mountain-stone available on the mud flats. Even sickles and roof nails were made of baked clay. Warka phase follows.
   * Genesis 11:4
     Protoliterate phase of city-states with temples, 'Come let us build a city' (c.3500 BC).
     Ziggurat building commences with heaven-temples at the apex. A ziggurat was a man-made mountain reflecting the mountain origin of the immigrants. Writing commences 3400 BC.

15 TABLETS TELL THEIR TALE

CHECKPOINTS

FURTHER ILLUSTRATED BY RECENT DISCOVERY

1. **Legal procedure**
   Hittite sale of cave and field to Abraham (Gen 23) is on legal terms practised in Abraham's time, 1900 BC (K.A. Kitchen, Liverpool University).

2. **Contemporary practice**
   In the time of Jacob, 1900 BC, Rachel took the family 'doll' or teraphim. The reason would not be known even to Moses. Archaeology reveals that the possession of the teraphim meant a right to a father-in-law's property.

3. **Literary style**
   Ugarit tablets, 1400 BC, showed the same style of poetry as in the Song of Miriam in Exodus 15.

4. **Educational methods**
   The Gezer calendar, 1000 BC, is a schoolboy's exercise tablet. It gives the annual farming rotation, and reflects Old Testament scripts of David's time.

5. **Parallel scripts**
   Samaritan Pentateuch (copies still exist) is found to be in the same style of script as the Siloam Inscription of Hezekiah's time, 721 BC, when the Samaritans were first taught the Torah.

6. Transmission accuracy

'The correct transmission of names is notoriously difficult.' Copies of Manetho's list of 140 Egyptian kings when compared with Egyptian monuments, has 63 of them unrecognisable in any single syllable. In contrast to this secular writer, 'the text in the Hebrew Bible has been transmitted with the most minute accuracy' (Dr J.W. Wenham, *Christ and the Bible*, T.P).

CHECKPOINTS

THE HUMAN AUTHORS OF THE OLD TESTAMENT

Time of writing according to evidences given in the manuscript

The Old Testament	Writer or Compiler	Date
The Pentateuch (Torah)	Written by Moses	14th–15th century BC
Joshua	Written by Phinehas, son of Aaron	c. 1380 BC
Judges to end of 2 Kings	Compiled by Jeremiah, Samuel and others	1050 BC onwards & c. 580 BC (Note 1)
The Latter Prophets (Isaiah, onwards)	By the Prophets named	8th–5th century BC
1 and 2 Chronicles to Esther	By Ezra and Nehemiah	5th century BC (Note 2)
Wisdom Literature	By those named	14th century BC to Exile

Note 1. Jeremiah used the contemporary accounts of Samuel 'who wrote the manner of the kingdom' 1,000 BC, Nathan, Gad, Ahijah, Iddo, Shemiah, Isaiah, and others of the School of the Prophets, and official royal court chronicles.

Note 2. They used the contemporary records of Shemiah and Iddo (2 Chron 13:22), Isaiah (2 Chron 26:22), Nathan, Ahijah and Iddo (2 Chron 9:29).

TWO ISAIAHS?

Two of the books of the prophets most attacked are Isaiah and Daniel.

The second half of Isaiah's work was attributed to another writer later. In this way the critics attempted to account for the fulfilment of the remarkable predictions of the emperor Cyrus. The critics did not believe that God could foretell and plan the future. Other critics even said there was a third Isaiah. But there are several clear indications of the unity of the whole book.

The unity of Isaiah

First there are over 300 words and expressions common to both sections – the former and latter part of Isaiah. Moreover, the Exile and return are not only written about in the second section but are also prophesied in the first section of Isaiah 11:11 onwards. (See also Isaiah's words to Hezekiah in 2 Kings 20:16–18.)

Second, there is a phrase quite peculiar to Isaiah which runs through the whole book and is equally distributed between the two supposed halves. (The chapters of the supposed first Isaiah are 1 to 39, and the supposed second Isaiah are chapters 40 to 66.) The phrase is 'The Holy One of Israel', referring to God. This occurs fourteen times in the first 39 chapters and sixteen times in the last 27 chapters, making a total of thirty. The phrase occurs only six times in the rest of the Old Testament, and four of these are in that part of history, 2 Kings 19, for which Isaiah would be responsible. The other two are in Jeremiah, the compiler of that history. The phrase is certainly the Isaiah hallmark throughout his book.

CHECKPOINTS

THE TRUTH OF THE TORAH

The Torah

The scroll called the Torah (Law) is Moses' work (Genesis to Deuteronomy). Called the Pentateuch when translated into Greek 288 BC at Alexandria, meaning: five books. It was one scroll before division. It can be seen that the end and the beginning of each was continuous originally.

So when in Deuteronomy 31:24, Moses finished writing the Torah, it was the **Pentateuch he placed in the Ark for safety.** Hilkiah re-discovered it in 731 BC (2 Chron 34:14–21).

Wellhausen (1860) said religion evolved; that it was not revealed to Moses as claimed.

So he reshuffled it (JEDP) and said it was not completed until 400 BC

Hittite legal code, 14th century BC, shows the Pentateuch was by Moses. Critics still ignore this, and still cut up text according to God's names.

Anthropologists (e.g. Professor Evans-Pritchard) and archaeologists found religion did not evolve.

Primitive belief in Creator, but degenerated to animism.

Professor F.K. Kitchen finds ancient authors use two names for God 'Yah' and 'El' in one text, e.g. Ebla tablets, so JEDP theory is wrong.

Torah copied for Samaritan immigrants in 722 BC.

So it existed before 400 BC. Their copy matches the style of Hezekiah's conduit tablet 701 BC.

Synagogues still keep their Torah scroll in an Ark cupboard, from Mosaic tradition.

Phinehas was Moses' scribe and records his death.

Themes in the Torah are worked out in the rest of the Bible. Finalised in Revelation.

SACRED SCRIPTURES

We know from experience that some whose faith has been strengthened by scientific evidence for the Bible have had that faith undermined later by a more subtle attack – criticism.

Paul Kanamori was a native of Japan. At school one of the boys found a Bible. He was fascinated as he read it without the help of a missionary or a commentary. He was converted to Jesus Christ. He could not keep the good news to himself, and so he let other boys in his school read it. Many were converted, and without any adult teachers they formed themselves into a fellowship, until they numbered 100. Their ages ranged from thirteen to eighteen years.

The joy of salvation took them into the market place to proclaim their good news.

Kanamori gradually took the leadership, but they were severely persecuted, and Kanamori was cast into prison. Although he was searched he hid the Gospels of Matthew and John in the inner lining of his waistcoat.

When he was released, he wanted to become a pastor, so he went to a theological college. There he was taught all the theories of Higher Criticism and sadly what persecution could not do, this subtle deception accomplished. He was taught that the Bible was only a collection of myths. God had not revealed his truth to the Old Testament prophets; religion had merely evolved; there was no Creator; and the resurrection was all imagination.

He lost his faith and for 24 years he continued in the darkness of unbelief. Then tragedy struck. His greatly loved wife died, leaving him with his nine children. He was shattered.

Then into his thoughts came scriptures he had learnt long ago. 'I am the resurrection and the life, says the Lord. He who believes on me, though he were dead, yet shall he live.'

He returned to the Saviour, and the old joy returned, and his eyes were opened to the clever deceptions which had tripped him up.

That same Higher Criticism is still taught today. It is compulsory for most of those on preachers' courses and is why you have the opportunity in this book of letting the Bible speak for itself.

CHECKPOINTS

THE BIBLE SPEAKS

1. **The Former Prophets:** Joshua to 2 Kings
   - The phrase 'Unto this Day' indicates contemporary recording: Rahab, rescued from Jericho 1400 BC, was still alive 'unto this day'. So the book of Joshua was recorded by a contemporary writer, see also Judges 1:21.
   - Jerusalem, so famous after David's kingship, was unknown when Judges was written (Jdg 19:10).
   - The contemporary writers from Samuel to 2 Chronicles are named six times. They were Samuel, Nathan, Gad and Ahijah, Iddo, Isaiah, etc.
   - The Bible history is not the secular history which has perished (1 Kgs 14:19) and which were the official court records, not Kings and Chronicles of our Bible. **Ezra named 22 writers of sacred history but knows nothing of supposed JEDP compilers.** Yet Ezra names everybody who did the least thing!
   - Evidence that Jeremiah used these writers to compile Judges to 2 Kings; e.g. 'Ears Tingle'. Phrases typical only of Jeremiah.

2. **The Latter Prophets:** Isaiah to Malachi
   - Nearly all give date and reign of their prophecy, yet higher critics usually say it was someone else living hundreds of years later pretending it was a prophecy. Why? Because they did not believe that God could foretell the future.
   - Yet this is what proves he is God according to Isaiah 46:9.

3. Isaiah
   - It enables Isaiah to prophesy Cyrus and Exile 200 years later, but a second Isaiah is postulated by critics as writing after the event which detailed analysis disproves.
   - Three hundred words common to all 66 chapters, and

phrase peculiar to Isaiah. 'Holy One of Israel' occurs equally throughout. Therefore only one author.

4. Daniel

- He notes who reigned when he wrote from 588 BC onwards, but critics say it was written after 165 BC when a prophecy was fulfilled.
- Yet Daniel had already been translated into Greek by 288 BC.

CHECKPOINTS

EXCITING DISCOVERIES OF THE EBLA TABLETS

1. Discovery in Syria has shown that the assumptions that different authors used separate names for the divinity are wrong. Individual tablets showed that the same author used more than one name for the divinity on the one tablet: Jehovah and Elohim were used by the same author on any one tablet. This was the news released to the world in 1977 by Professor Pettinato.

2. The Eblate empire commenced about 3500 BC and the tablets which Pettinato has been translating date at 2300 BC. There are 17,000, each about 1 sq ft (35 x 30 cm). Each contains about 6,000 words.
   K.A. Kitchen of Liverpool University points out the names of God (El) and Jehovah (Yah) alternate as names of God in the work of the same scribe. (Yaw is an abbreviated form of Yahweh.)

3. Arthur Gibson of Manchester University points out: the use of these two names is not an indication of different authorship or of later sources.
   The one author, Moses, would quite naturally follow the literary methods of his time and use both names in their related texts.
   This proves that the documentary theory is quite unscientific and wrong.

4. Some have objected that Moses could not have recorded his own burial in the last note at the end of Deuteronomy. All ancient writers had their scribes and Moses' scribe Phinehas would add this.

16 **A**BRAHAM'S ARMY

Q *What was Abraham doing with a private army?*

Well, these tablets which have been found are called the Execration Texts. First they throw light on the meaning of a word in Genesis. It is 'Hanikim'. Men of influence had them. They were retainers or private soldiers. They would have regular inspections.

One tablet records an inspection of private armies which took place in the city of Ur, Abraham's city. This was in 2000 BC – the time of Abraham. The tablet shows that others had small private armies too; it gives a list of them. The smallest was 40 soldiers and the largest was 600. So that means that Abraham's army of 318 was about average in size (Genesis 14:14).

Archaeology has opened up a whole new vista of Abraham's culture.

Abraham would regard himself as a modern, educated man of his day. The idea that many had of Abraham as a primitive bedouin chief with a few sheep and goats nibbling at his tent pegs, has been changed by archaeological discovery. Thousands of tablets have now been deciphered which give us a very full picture of life 2000 years BC. We have more detailed knowledge of those times than we have even of medieval England!

Thirty thousand Accadian and Sumerian tablets descibe children's education, their mathematics, spelling tablets and work schedules, and nearly 2,000 children's 'text books' have been found in the form of tablets written by the children. History, religion and mathematics were taught.

Advanced systems of calculation included adding columns of 60. This value column system made our modern calculators possible, and the figure 60 persists on our watches still, giving us 60 seconds to the minute and 60 minutes to the hour. The circle was 360°.

DONKEYS VERSUS 'ROLLS-ROYCE' 2000 BC

I have told you about Abraham's private army, which protected his transport business. What were these caravans like and how were supplies maintained?

The size, numbers and system are surprising. Dr Dent says,

There are Syrian records of caravan trains with 3,000 donkeys! There was an elaborate maintenance system. Grass was planted along the trails to feed the pack animals. People were employed to make specially-terraced fields. They had to fetch water and lived in beehive-shaped houses along the routes. The caravan donkey was a particular breed. It could travel for two or three days without water while carrying a pack weighing 150–200 lbs. One man would control five donkeys and walk behind his charges, but the leader would ride on a donkey.

Camels were also in use in Abraham's time. A certain commentator did not know this and thought that the association of camels with Abraham was an anachronism.

Bones of domesticated camels 2000 BC have now been found, but the camel was a prestige symbol, only ridden by the general manager. It was his 'Rolls-Royce'. When Abraham's steward journeyed north to 'Crossroads', to find a suitable bride for his master's son, Isaac, it was his master's 'Rolls-Royce' camels he took. He would only have donkeys for himself. 'The servant took ten camels, of the camels of his master, and he departed' (Gen 24:10, RSV).

Fig. 15. Restoration of a two-storey house of the time of Abraham in the town of Ur, 2,000 BC. This demonstrates the advanced development of civilisation and habitation with bathrooms, drainage (linked to town drains) and second storeys for servant accommodation.

Courtesy: Sir Leonard Woolley, Ur of the Chaldees, *Pelican Books, 1952*

CHECKPOINTS

'ROLLS-ROYCE CAMELS', 2000 BC

1. **The Bible dates make harmony with history:**
   Some commentators give dates 200 years later than Bible
   dates and then accuse the Bible of not matching history.

2. **Tablets found testify the truth of:**
   Abraham's private army parade (Ur).
   Abraham's business.
   Abraham's mortgage risk – Eliezer (Gen 15:2).
   Abraham's family international transport company.
   Four kings versus five is an historical fact.
   Deeds on the doll for Rachel. Legal knowledge lost later.
   Court cases at city gates.

3. **Camels were the 'Rolls-Royce' of the bosses**
   Only donkeys for employees.

4. **Abraham's advanced civilisation 2000 BC**
   Algebra and arithmetic for Abram at Ur.
   The proof: 60 secs; 60 mins; 360 degrees on our watches and
   compasses, come from Ur.

THE RUINS OF SODOM AND GOMORRAH TELL THEIR STORY

A convincing instance is the geological history of Sodom and
Gomorrah, past, present and future. The first reference to
Sodom comes early in Scripture. Turn to it in Genesis 10:19. It
refers to Sodom and the cities of this Dead Sea valley as the area
of prime beauty and productivity which was inhabited by the
descendants of Noah's son Ham. In this verse there is no hint of
the destruction to come in the days of Abraham. We can there-

fore reasonably conclude that the source of this information is prior even to Abraham himself

City of the Dead Sea

Remember that the Lord punished Sodom for its homosexuality by making fire and sulphur rain down from the sky. Jesus said it would be a problem soon before his return, but he can help sufferers.

As I have said, if you go down to the Dead Sea, you can see the evidence for the destruction of that city of Sodom. If you walk round the southern end you can pick up lumps of sulphur even today, and the salt which rained down and engulfed Lot's wife can be seen around on the peaks and rocks. They are encrusted with salt!

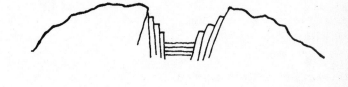

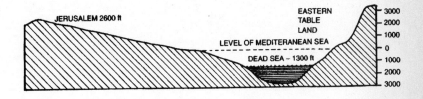

Fig. 16. The cross-section of a typical rift valley and the rift of the Jordan Valley to scale.

There is a salt mountain with a 150-foot thick stratum of salt. The earthquake ruptured this and the fierce volcanic fire would melt it as it shot up into the air and rained down its terrible death upon those who disbelieved God's warning.

You can also see the bitumen if you paddle in the Dead Sea at some spots. This tar, melted by volcanic heat, rained down all aflame.

Sodom and the Jordan valley were at the northern end of that great rift valley which runs south down into Africa. In that same rift valley in Africa, there are lakes of tar. A lot of our motoring roads are made from it.

The extraordinary experience of this rift valley is featured throughout times, in Ezekiel, and to the last days in Revelation. God knows beforehand when these geological events are going to happen!

First we have a description of its beauty long before Moses. Where did this information come from? Perhaps it was handed down from Abraham. Archaeology has found evidence which confirms that the area was extremely fertile before the overthrow of Sodom and Gomorrah. Beneath the barren sterile soft soils of the surface there is a thick layer of rich soil.

17   GOD THE GEOLOGIST

Another example of God's 'incidental geology' is in Isaiah 40:12 where God says he 'weighed the mountains on the scales and the hills in a balance' (NIV). This is called 'isostasy'. The height of the hills and mountains is counterbalanced by the depth of the 'root' of the elevated area. The 'root' goes down deeper into the sima of the plastic crust and remains balanced by its weight.

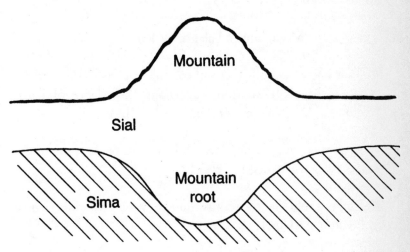

Fig. 17. An example of isostasy in which the upthrust of a mountain is counterbalanced by a 'root' protruding into the sima.

We have already seen that the Bible indicates that life is created by God's words, the DNA code, and how Psalm 139 refers to the genetic Book of Man. We have also read God's explanation to Job (chap 38) of what makes the sun rise, namely the earth turning on an axis described in the Bible as like a Babylonian clay cylinder on a spindle.

CHECKPOINTS

GOD THE GEOLOGIST: USEFUL LIST OF PROOFS

1. God gives correct order of events.
   Supported from Astrophysics and fossils.

2. God tells three prophets of rift valley events to come (Joel, Ezekiel and Zechariah).

3. God tells Job that the earth turns on an axis and hangs on nothing (Job 38:12–14).

4. How God made valleys into mountains (Is 40)
   • by weathering (v 4)
   • by synclines
   • isostasy 'Mountains in balance' (v 12).

5. Jesus knew that at his second coming in parts of the world it would be night, morning, afternoon [knowledge of Earth globe] (Lk 17:34–36; Mt 24:39–42 KJV).

6. Jesus knew nuclear fission would come through uranium. So did Peter [elements] (2 Pet 3:12).

7. Paul was told that the resurrection body was an atomic change 'in atom' (1 Cor 15:52).

8. Quantam physics 'By him all things hold together' (Col 1:17).

9. Visible things were created by 99% invisible according to quantum mechanics (Heb 11:3).

MOSES VINDICATED

One of the things that one critic said in his TV series, was that there was no evidence that Israel came out of Egypt in the year 1250 BC. That's the event that we call the Exodus. He said that the whole story is fictional. It never happened.

Of course it didn't. Not in 1250 BC anyway. You see, the Bible says it happened 200 years earlier. If people don't take the Bible's dates to guide them, they are bound to get things wrong. The Bible says it took place in 1440 BC. If you accept the Bible date, you will find that all the events of Exodus in the Bible slot into the framework of Egyptian history marvellously.

This is the kind of circular argument which is typical of the sceptics. They manufacture their own contradictions and then accuse the Bible of them.

Q *Where in the Bible does it say that the Exodus happened in 1440 BC?*

There are two or three places describing the Exodus; 1 Kings 6:1 says that Solomon started to build the temple 480 years after the Israelites escaped from Egypt. The date of Solomon's temple was 960 BC 'even sceptics agree with that date'. Add 480 to 960 BC and that gives you the date of the Exodus as 1440 BC. Now if those critics started with the Bible date, they would find that Egyptian history not only fits in, it explains why Moses ran away from Egypt at the age of 40, why he returned 40 years later, who the Pharaohs were, and the archaeology slots into the whole framework. The whole list of dates and events in the Bible harmonises perfectly.

CHECKPOINTS

CRITICS DEBATE

1. Three TV programmes ignore information and biblical alignment:

Bible	Egyptian Archaeology
Joseph	Foreign Shepherd Kings
Slavery	Nationals gain throne 18th Dynasty
Moses Adopted	By Princess Hatshepsut (Thotmes III)
Moses flees	Hatshepsut had died
Exodus	Amenhetep II
1st born death	Thotmes IV not the heir
Conquest 1400	Amenhetep III (Akhnaton) ignores appeals found on Amarna tablets

2. Three days' journey to Hatshepsut's temple for Moses.
   Moses' Hebrew name 'Manasse' inscribed.
   'Drawn out' is meaning of 'Moses' on tablet.

3. Hasty entombment of Amenhetep II
   Sphinx slab by Thotmes IV testimony (after Exodus) critics wrong reckoning.
   'You are idle' on Egyptian mural (cf. Ex 5:17).

4. Beetle symbol (Scarab) = Egypt (British Museum).
   Reduces Palestine resistance to Israel's conquest.
   (Ex 23:28; Deut 7:20 'Hornet').

5. Amenhetep III brings monotheism to Egypt (cf. above).

6. Experts in archaeology reject lack of knowledge of some Higher Critics.

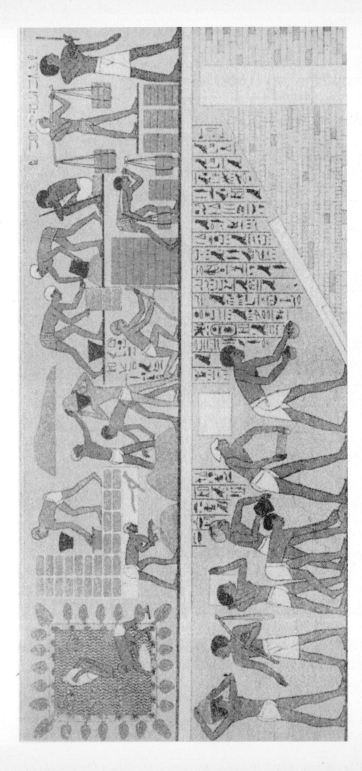

Fig. 18. Evidence of the Hebrew slaves in Egypt. Egyptian mural of Moses' time contains the words: 'You are idle! You are idle!' In Exodus 5:8 and 17, these words are spoken by Pharaoh about the Hebrew brickmakers, and when telling the slavedrivers to be more severe.

Courtesy: Story of the Bible, Fleetway House, London

18 THE IMPACT OF ISRAEL

A reviewer said that there are no monuments either in Egypt or Palestine that refer to Israel. But this is not correct. It should be realised that none of the Egyptian monuments ever refer to a defeat. Consequently, the escape of the slaves is sarcastically recorded as the 'escape of lepers'. Moreover, the entry into Palestine is recorded on the Tel Amarna tablets. The Caananites had been appealing for help from the Pharaoh Akhnaton, to stop the Israelite invasion. They say that if he doesn't help, the whole of the land will be overrun.

A DESPERATE PLEA FOR HELP

Here it is – a loyal soldier called Abdkhiba writes about Jerusalem to Egypt. He wrote to this Pharaoh Akhnaton:

> The king's whole land will be lost. Behold the territory of Seir as far as Carmel, its princes are wholly lost and hostility prevails against me. [He has appealed apparently several times, for he goes on] If no troops come this year, the whole territory of my Lord the king will perish. [Then he appeals that the king will at least send forces to ensure the retreat of himself and his men doesn't happen, and in a postscript he adds to Akhnaton's secretary] Bring these words plainly before my lord the king. The whole land of my lord the King is going to ruin.

The tablets say that the Hebrews were invading from Seir and Edom and the Bible says that that is where the Israelites launched their invasion. You find the details in Deuteronomy 2.

Q *Did Pharaoh Akhnaton actually send his army to help the Caananites?*
No, he didn't, and there is a good reason why he didn't.

He knew now that the Pharaohs could not fight against God. The ten plagues and the crossing of the Red Sea and the miraculous drying up of the River Jordan had proved that.

THE LAMB AND THE LINTEL

The tenth plague, however – the death of the firstborn – has no natural explanation. God moved in a token judgement against sin, fearfully demonstrating what the wages of sin are. For all who would believe and obey, there was a graciously provided means of escape – the Passover. In every household there would be one death – either that of the firstborn, or that of the divinely-appointed substitute lamb.

Q *Why were both lamb and lintel needed to deliver Israel from Egypt?*

Look at the lamb first. In how many ways did the lamb fore-shadow Christ? First, God said the lamb must be perfect. It must have no blemishes. This depicted Jesus who was without sin or blemish. That is why he could die in the sinner's place.

Second, the lamb must be slain. So the Lord Jesus was killed for us. His blood atoned for our sins, 'Behold the Lamb of God which takes away the sin of the world,' said John the Baptist.

Was the lintel, the top of a door frame also necessary? Israel was not delivered from Egypt because of their nationality. They were delivered because they applied blood to the lintel. God said that anyone who did not apply the blood, was to die when the angel of death passed over the land. If an Israelite did not apply the blood of the sacrificed lamb, he died despite his nationality. Also, any Egyptian who applied the blood would be saved. In fact, there was a mixed host who came out of Egypt with the Israelites. So you see, it was the lamb and the lintel. It was not sufficient for the lamb to be slain, the person had to spread the precious blood onto the lintel post of the door of his house.

THE CROSSING OF THE JORDAN

On one occasion when I was going along the Jordan valley, I took a photo of the place where the River Jordan got blocked off. Jordan ceased to flow when steep soft banks collapsed, just as Joshua reported.

Just think about that for a moment. It shows God's control

over natural events. God was actually telling Joshua before it happened that the banks would collapse just at the right moment, just as the ark of the covenant was approaching the flood waters. The waters would shrink away just at the speed with which the priests marched forwards with the ark.

As I stood there, I imagined Joshua also standing there and writing in his report those words in chapter 3:16:

> The waters which came down from above stood and rose up upon a heap not far from the city called Adam, that is beside Zaretan, and those waters which came down toward the Dead Sea were cut off.

Did you know that the same thing happened in 1927? Sir Charles Marston tells you in his book, *The Bible Comes Alive,* that an earthquake shook Palestine in 1927? This made those soft banks collapse as they did in Joshua's day. This made Jordan dry up for 22 hours. That would give ample time for the armies of Israel to cross over and camp at Gilgal, ready to attack Jericho.

S.O.S.

Archaeology has revealed something not recorded in Scripture. The alarmed kings in Canaan sent urgent requests for help to Pharaoh of Egypt. Their letters or tables were found in his record office. As we saw, they are called 'the Tel el Amarna Tablets'. They were found by an old peasant woman in Egypt when she was rummaging in the ruins. They are dated between 1400 and 1360 BC. That time fits in perfectly. The Israelites are called Hebrews, but pronounced 'Habiru'. Notice that Pharaoh knows them as Hebrews in Exodus 7:16.

Here are some of the cries asking for Pharaoh's help:

1. 'The land of Shechem has gone over to the Hebrews'.
   Shechem was where Joshua read out the blessings and cursings from Deuteronomy as God instructed.
2. Another extract from the king of Sidon reads: 'Behold all my

cities which the Pharaoh has given into my hands have fallen into the hands of the Hebrews.'

3. Another king (of Gebal) wrote: 'He has conquered lands are for this Hebrew, so now there is none who is a friend to me.'

CHECKPOINTS

MIRACLE TIME

1. Three main miracle periods – Exodus, Elijah, Emanuel

2. Ten Plagues. Ten years natural calamities happen together in months (but 'first-born' fatalities were supernatural). Sphinx slab evidence to Pharaoh's first-born fatality.

3. The God of Nature:
   Red Sea recession by gale (Ex 14:21).
   Jordan dammed up by soft soil slip (Josh 3:13–16).
   It happened again in 1927 – Jordan blocked for 22 hours.

4. Jericho's mound and 'The spy who loved me'.
   Amarna tablets plea for help 1400 BC.
   Tablets ignored – Pharaoh frightened of Jehovah Canaanites' cruelty to children.
   Rahab ancestress to the Redeemer (Mt 1:5).

19 THE LONG DAY SUBSTANTIATED

Herodotus, the great historian of ancient times, tells you that the priests of Egypt showed him in their records the existence of an unusually long day.

There are six independent records by ancient nations of this long day. The Indian Hindu account says, 'In the life of Chrishnu, the sun delayed setting to hear the pious ejaculations of Akroon; that planet went down to make a difference of about twelve hours'. The date? It corresponds with Joshua's date (about 1400 BC)!

Professor Totten has stated that research shows that a whole day of 24 hours has been inserted into the world's history. Professor Totten has found that the sun and moon have only been in that juxtaposition once. I quote,

> . . . by taking the equinoxes, eclipses and transits, and working backwards to the winter solstice of Joshua's day, it is found to fall on Wednesday, whereas by calculating forwards to the winter solstice of Joshua's day, it is found to fall on a Tuesday. So a whole day of 24 hours has been inserted into the world's history.

So Professor Totten affirms that 'not before or since has there been a date which will harmonise with the required relative positions of the sun, moon and earth as conditioned in the Holy Scripture'.

The Superintendent of Greenwich Observatory noted, from Joshua 10:12–13, that the sun was at midday and the moon at the horizon – the valley – north-west at Aijalon. With this astronomical information, he was able to project back and find that it happened on the 21st July.

E.W. Maunder, Fellow of the Royal Astronomical Society,

late of the Royal Observatory Greenwich, wrote about the subject and traces not only the actual spot on which Joshua must have been standing at the time, but the date and time of the day when this remarkable phenomenon took place. Does the Bible give so much detail? Yes! Joshua 10:12 says, 'Sun, stand thou still at Gibeon, and thou moon, over the valley of Aijalon.' You see, the Bible is so accurate that it tells you the actual position of the sun and moon in the sky at the time.

The scripture says that the sun stood still for about a whole day, so that would mean nearly 24 hours. Astonomers find that a day has been added to the astronomical calendar. The final 40 minutes or so (10 degrees) would be that added as a sign to Hezekiah, in 2 Kings 20:10.

CHECKPOINTS

JOSHUA'S LONG DAY

He said, 'Sun, stand thou still over Gibeon and thou moon over the valley of Aijalon.'

They obeyed and the sun stopped in mid-sky for nearly a whole day. How's that for a *Guinness Book of Records* entry? As a matter of fact, it was recorded in the *Guinness Record Book* of that day. It was called the 'Book of Jashver'.

Reasons for the Long Day

Enemy rushing to city safety.

Joshua not equipped for siege warfare.

Jashver, The Guinness Record book of ancient times Joshua 10:13; 2 Samuel 1:18.

Records of Long Day

Herodotus 500 BC and Egyptian records.

Indian Chrishnu account.

Other ancient records – China, Aboriginal, American Indians.

Professor Totten's equinoxes, eclipses and transits.

Superintendent of Greenwich Observatory, 21st July.

Position of moon and sun (Josh 10:12).

E.W. Maunder, Royal Astronomical Society.

How?

Sir Ambrose Fleming and 'Krypton Factor'.

Comet influence and meteorites.

Other notes

Rahab was still alive when Joshua was written (Josh 6:25) – Phinehas, Moses' and Joshua's secretary (Josh 24:33).

Table of time

1400 BC Bible date for the Long Day. 300 Years to Jeptha (Jdg 11:26). 180 Years Jeptha to Solomon. From 1 Kgs 6:1.

20 TABLETS AND TEMPLE

Tablets found actually describe the transport of timbers from King Hiram to the Temple of Solomon. Hiram was a Phoenician and these records were written by a man named Sanchuniathon. He says that King Hiram transported timbers and planks on 8,000 camels.

Q But hang on a minute, Victor. A critic said that camels weren't in use until 360 years later than this.

This tablet proves this record is true and critics wrong, doesn't it? Think of it! Eight thousand camels to transport cedars to the temple building project. Now listen to the equivalent account in the Bible. It's in 1 Kings 5:6: 'Solomon said, instruct the cedars of Lebanon be cut for me for no one among us knows how to cut timber like you people of Tyre.' Hiram replied 'I'm ready to do all that you desire in the matter of cedar and cyprus timber.'

Q But what do the tablets add to the information in the Bible?

They give the actual names of those mariners. There were Kedorus, Jaminus and Kotilus. They also say that Hiram sent highly-skilled bronze workers to Solomon's Temple. One such worker is mentioned here in 1 Kings 7:13, I quote, 'He was the son of a widow of the tribe of Naphtali and his father was a man of Tyre, a worker in bronze, very skilful for bronze work. He came to King Solomon and did all his work' (RSV).

The Ras Shamra tablets from the coast of Syria are poems and psalms about David's time and of course the wisdom of Solomon who was famous for his proverbs and natural history. Solomon was also a great expert on horses. He imported them from a place which the Bible calls 'Que'. We've only learnt recently that this was a place away in Asia Minor (Turkey). This was where the famous horse culture of the Hittites arose; they took to breeding white horses. One white horse was worth four times as much as an Egyptian horse. You can imagine Solomon riding a great white horse.

CHECKPOINTS

SOLOMON'S EMPIRE

1. **Two critics say there is no evidence of Solomon's buildings. The reason:**
   'Not one stone left' at Jerusalem's prophesied fall in AD 70 but Solomon's casemate style visible at: Gezer, Hazor,
   Megiddo Forts (A Millard, Liverpool University).
   Phoenician materials (2 Chron 2) confirmed.

2. **Camel blunder by critic who said they were not used until 601 BC**
   Corrected by experts:
   - Professor Zeuner – camels domesticated in Abraham's time 2000 BC.
   - Sanchuniathon says Solomon's transport had 8,000 camels! He confirms all the details of 1 Kings 5:8–11.
   - Professor Kitchen lists evidence 2000–1400 BC.

3. **Ingots from India**
   Confirmed by Jerome and Greek Septuagint.

4. **Critics should take 'tablets' to correct scepticism**
   - Hiram of Tyre confirms temple materials.
   - Hiram sent experienced sailors.
   - David's psalms style on Ras Shamra tablets.
   - Solomon's horses from 'Que' Turkey (Ras Samra tablets).
   - Solomon's stables unearthed at Gezer, Hazor, Megiddo.
   - Bible lists cities Israel failed to capture.

CHECKPOINTS

JOSHUA TO SOLOMON

A. 300 years from the conquest to Jeptha's first year

West of Jordan	No. of yrs	East of Jordan	No. of yrs
Joshua and Elders	20		
Mesopotamian oppression	8		
Rest (Othniel) – Judges 3:11	40		
Moabite oppression – Judges 3:14	18		
Ehud and Shamgar – Judges 3:28–4:1	80		
Sisera's oppression – Judges 4:3	20		
Deborah and Barak – Judges 5:1,31	40		
Midianite oppression – Judges 6:1	7		
Gideon – Judges 8:28	40		
Abimelech – Judges 9:22	3		
Jair's era – Judges 10:3	22		
Tola of Ephraim – Judges 10:2	23		
Ammonite invasion of W Jordan after 18 years in E Jordan – Judges 10:9	1	Ammonite oppression in E Jordan ending with the invasion of W Jordan	18
Jeptha's total – Judges 11:26 TOTAL	300	since 2^1/$_2$ tribes entered East Jordan	

The problem now is in accounting for the remaining 180 years between Jeptha and Solomon, to bring the total to 480 years (1 Kgs 6:1). There are two factors to note, the first is that the Philistine oppression runs concurrently with Samson and Eli Judgeship. This is clear from Judges 13:1; 15:11, 20 and 16:31. The second is that the duration of Saul's reign is unknown in the Old Testament record. The 180 years work out thus:

B. 180 years between Jeptha and Solomon

Jeptha – Judges 12:7	5	
Ibzan of Bethlehem – Judges 12:9	7	
Elon – Judges 12:11	10	
Abdon – Judges 12:14	8	
Samson – Judges 15:20; 16.31	20	Note 1
Eli – 1 Samuel 4:18	40	
Samuel – 1 Samuel 7:2; 14:18	20	Note 2
Saul (by deduction)	27	Note 3
David – 2 Samuel 5:4,5	40	Note 4
Solomon to 4th year – 1 Kings 6:1	3	
TOTAL	180	
Plus 300 to Jeptha	300	
GRAND TOTAL	480	
(I Kings 6:1)		

Note 1. Philistine oppression of 40 years runs concurrently with Samson and part of Eli's judgeship.

Note 2. Unlikely to be longer as Samuel was a boy in Eli's 40 years and did not die until the end of Saul's reign.

Note 3. At Saul's death, David and Jonathan were about 30 years old (2 Sam 5:4,5) therefore were teenagers together 15 years earlier when Saul had reigned 12 years. Jonathan would be about three years old when Saul was crowned (say at the age of 23 years – married at 19).

Note 4. Saul would be 50 when slain: men usually ceased to go into battle after 50 years of age.

21 THE FALKLANDS JONAH

There are on record three or four cases of seamen who have been swallowed by a whale and survived. One was an Arab from Kuwait who fortunately had his sharp dagger with him. With this he cut a way out of the stomach and escaped. Another case is the Falklands Jonah. His name was James Bartley and he was swallowed by a whale, but survived to tell his story.

He was a member of a whaling crew on the ship *Star of the East*. The crew sighted a spout of water coming out of the sea and knew it was from a whale. They gave chase and when they were near enough, fired a harpoon. In the effort, Bartley fell overboard and, in spite of a search, he was nowhere to be seen. Eventually, after half a day trying to get the poor whale on board, they managed to haul it up and land it on the deck. By this time it was dead.

They cut open the stomach and out fell James Bartley, unconscious. They threw a bucket of sea-water over him to restore his consciousness. When he came round he was raving mad. His skin had been parched to a deadly white by the gastric juices of the whale.

He had been in the whale's stomach for nearly a day. When he recovered sanity, he said that inside the whale he had plenty of air but it was very hot. He fainted from fear, not from lack of air. The whale was of the cachalot species which has no grill in its mouth and is able to swallow even sharks. It often vomits up contents of its stomach onto the shore, just as Jonah was vomited up.

Another case was Marshall Jenkins who was a crew member of a USA whaling boat. This was before the harpoon gun had been invented and so the harpooner stood in the bows with a spear poised and thrust it into the whale. Its immediate reaction

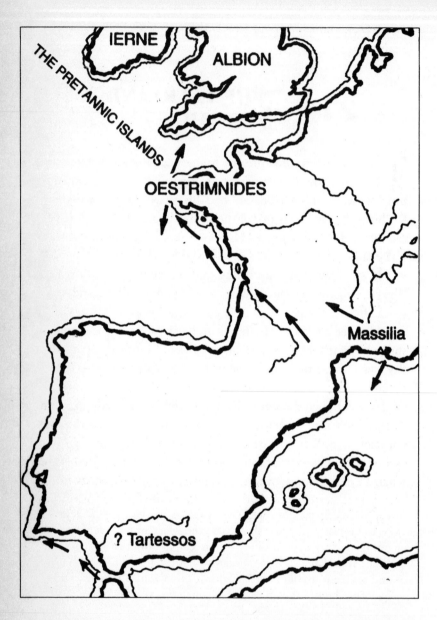

Fig. 19. Ancient Tarshish: Jonah's escape route in the ancient world. Tartessos or Tarshish was near Gibraltar, which was a port of call on the way to Brittany (Oestrimnides) and the Western Isles. A stop would also be made at Marseilles (Massilia).

was to turn and capsize the boat with its powerful tail. All hands were flung into the sea and Martin Jenkins was swallowed up. After many hours the injured whale came up to the surface and in its death struggles it brought up its last meal, as frequently happens. Among the mess of cuttlefish and octopas tentacles was Jenkins who had been able to breath in the Whale's stomach without damage.

Jonah thought God could not bring him back from a paid-up passenger spot in the sun on a cruise to sunny Spain. But that is where he underestimated God's natural resources. God had already created an air-conditioned submarine sea mammal. Jonah was going to have a whale of a time learning to pray down on the ocean floor, 'I cried to you out of the belly of hell!' Dear me, Jonah, what language!

DR LAYARD FINDS NINEVEH

But the usual doubters doubted the story of Jonah, not only about the whale, but also what the Bible said of the size of this immense city, Nineveh. It was three days' journey in breadth. This was nearly 800 BC and was about 100 miles NNW of Baghdad. Dr Layard was a Higher Critic at first. He accepted without question all that criticsm asserted. He believed that the story of Jonah was only a myth with a moral. Archaeology had hardly started to correct corrupting concepts. Then Dr Layard made an expedition to ancient Nineveh and excavated its ruins. The public were astonished when he wrote his famous book *Nineveh and its Remains*. He found that Nineveh was all that the Bible said it was. I quote Jonah 3:3:

> Nineveh was an exceedingly great city, three days' journey in breadth and Jonah began to go into the city, going a day's journey, and he shouted, 'In 40 days' time Nineveh will be destroyed by God.'

On page 336 of his book, Layard says, concerning the extent of the city,

> The dimensions of the city were 150 stadia for the two longest sides of the quadrangle, and 90 for the shortest, the square being 480 stadia or almost 60 miles . . . The three days' journey of Jonah should

correspond exactly with 60 miles of the square formed by the great ruins . . . 20 miles a day's journey in the East, and we have therefore exactly three days' journey.

Layard found that Nineveh was indeed a 'mighty city'. Its walls were huge like Babylon's. The inner wall was 76 feet high and 32 feet thick. That is wide enough for four traffic lanes – the motorway of ancient times, like an M25 around the outskirts. It provided the possibility for chariot races upon the walls, with 1,500 towers 200 feet high dominating the whole complex at regular intervals.

Bas relief sculptures on the walls show what a powerful culture it was – soldiers and chariots, shields and projectiles. But what is this low relief on the wall – **a man looking out of the mouth of a fish** – could it be Jonah? Who knows.

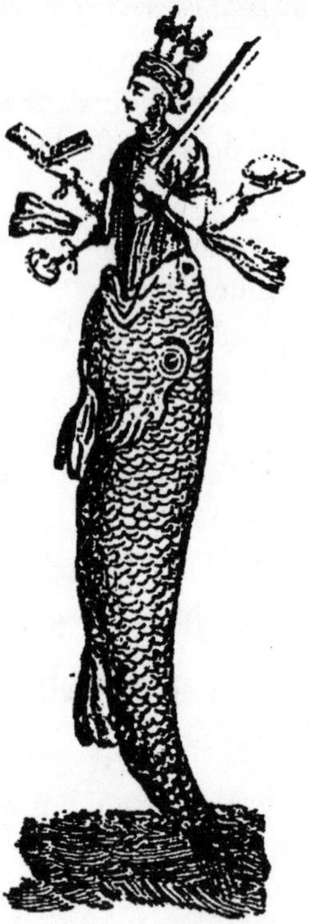

Fig. 20. **Fish god Nina**. Found on a wall in Nineveh. The city was named after the god Nina. Jonah, who came out of the belly of a 'big fish' would have frightening portent for Ninevites.

CAN YOU SWALLOW JONAH?

If ever there was a book in the Bible which was unlikely to be true, it is the book of the Prophet Jonah. Yet all its impossibilities have now been proved factual. Here is that list:

1. That Jonah was swallowed by a whale and coughed up alive
2. That passengers did pay fares for a sea trip as far as Gibraltar.
3. That God had created a sea mammal able to swallow Jonah and keep him alive.
4. That Nineveh was an exceeding huge city of 60 miles across ('3 days' journey').

5. That Jonah's strange appearance would compel the ruling despot to accept warning.
6. That God had a plant which could grow up in one night and wither away the next morning.
7. That Jehovah God was a God of love who wants to spare the children and cattle of cruel foreigners.

Some have even questioned whether Jonah existed: 2 Kings 14:25 states clearly that he did. 'God spoke by the hand of his servant Jonah', in the reign of the northern Israel king Jeroboam II. He was contemporary with Hosea about 765 BC.

Can you swallow Jonah? I thank God for my scientific training, for it is precisely because of it that I can reaffirm the truth of Jonah and the Bible.

CHECKPOINTS

JONAH – USEFUL POINTS

1. Cachelot whales can and have swallowed a man, e.g. James Bartley
   Mystery of when and why whale was created.
   Jonah's parched appearance would frighten superstitious tyrant.

2. Passenger sea trips featured in ancient times.
   Pictures on Nineveh's walls.

3. Sceptics doubted Nineveh's size until Layard excavated it (60 miles in diameter).
   Walls 76 feet high, 32 feet thick.

4. Palmcrist plant does grow and wither rapidly.

5. God revealed his love in Old Testament very early, e.g. Exodus 20:6 (cf. Jonah 4:2); 1 Kings 21:25–29; Psalm 18:6,18; Jeremiah 9:23,24; Lamentations 3:23; Hosea 2:20.

22 THE GREAT CRISES

Dr Dent comments, 'It may have been in the plain between the Tower of Babylon and the Palace of Nebuchadnezzar that the "image of gold" was set up.' This statue was 100 feet high and 10 feet wide and was a representation of himself which was to be worshipped. Records tell us that Nebuchadnezzar made public use of worshipping statues not only in Babylon , but also in Ur.

When the three Hebrew children refused to bow down to this image, they were punished by being thrown into a fiery furnace. Excavators at Babylon have found a furnace with the inscription, 'This is the place of burning where men who blasphemed the gods of Chaldea die by fire'. Also, a ruined college library was discovered revealing curricula for native princes. They were instructed and trained especially for 'Interpretations of dreams and visions'. 'Impiety to any gods – cast alive into a fiery furnace' and 'Untoward acts relative to a king – cast alive into the den of lions'.

For centuries the site of Babylon has lain waste. Critics thought that the Bible's description was a myth until archaeology revealed an amazing metropolis.

Dr Dent sums up the archaeologist's discoveries:

In the days of Nebuchadnezzar, the city of Babylon was large and grand. The walls were 60 miles in circumference, 80 feet thick and 300 feet high and its foundations went down 35 feet. Around its walls were 250 towers used as guard rooms. Surrounding the city was a moat and in the wall were 100 gates of brass. The city was divided almost in half by the river Euphrates and 25 gates connecting streets with ferry boats. Over the river was a bridge with stone piers half a mile long and 30 feet wide. At night drawbridges were removed. A feat of ancient engineering was the tunnel which went under the river and was 15 feet wide and 12 feet high. The walls were so wide that chariot races were a common occurrence and it is claimed that four chariots in line would race around the city on the wall.

CHECKPOINTS

GREAT CRISES

1. **The Elijah crisis** (answered by special miracles).
   Jezebel replaced Jehovah by Baal horrors.
   Baal's castle at Mt Carmel 'carved by fire' (Dr Dent) Elijah challenges 850 there. Shows fire comes from Jehovah.
   Water in drought: 12 barrels poured over sacrifice!
   Palestine government survey reveals artesian basin with three and a half years supply; outlets at Carmel and Beersheba.

2. **The Daniel crisis**
   Ten days' test passed with credit.
   Feet of clay image prophesied. 2,500 years of history.
   Evidence for furnace furore
   Inscription 'This is the place of burning'.
   Penalty for impiety – cast alive in furnace fire.
   Training curricula for native princes (Dr Dent).
   Area cleared for mass worship (Leo Woolley).

3. **Babylon**
   Historical record and writing on the wall.
   City fell 16th October 539 BC.
   Repeated in 1988 to Ayatollah – glowing cross.
   Daniel third in kingdom. Discovered that Belshazzar was vice-regent.
   Critics thought Babylon a myth.
   Digs confirm. Walls 80 feet wide, 300 feet high 250 towers,

100 gates of brass.
Impressive main entrance.

4. **The book of Daniel**
   Critics wrong on Aramaic, but still ignore discoveries. Aramaic
   spoken 200 years before Daniel (Dan 8–12 in Aramaic).
   Daniel wrote 588 BC but critics date it 165 BC because of
   unbelief in prophecy.
   Greek translation made 100 years before critics' date!

23 WHY QUESTION THE VIRGIN BIRTH?

Why is Scripture so outspoken about the necessity of the virgin birth? Only the God–man could be a sufficient payment for sin or substitute for sinners like you and me – we who have done wrong in God's sight. It was essential for your salvation and mine. That is why the angel told Joseph to name the Child Jesus which means Saviour, because he will save his people from their sins (Mt 1:21).

The cross and the virgin birth are immediately tied together here. One cannot be effective without the other.

But what is the real reason why some question the virgin birth? It is because they do not believe in miracles. The Lord said beware of the yeast of deception of the Sadducees. He warned us that such unbelief would come into the church later.

Now we are clearly told in Acts 23:8 what kind of unbelief this is. The Sadducean religion did not believe in miracles.

Modern genetics reveal that the pairs of genes (alleles) from both parents make one person at conception. The statement 'That which is conceived in her is of the Holy Spirit', shows how God was the Father and the virgin Mary the mother. Also, the fact that DNA is a code demonstrates how the speech, or 'Word' of God, recorded upon the nucleic acids, would form the real genetic contribution from the Divine side. We see how Christ was fully and truly man, and yet not two natures, but God–man, not God and man, thus illustrating physically what had been arrived at theologically by earlier divines.

Yet ultimately our only authoritative source for the doctrine of the Incarnation is still the revelation of God in Holy Scripture.

CHECKPOINTS

VIRGIN CONCEPTION

1. **A sacred subject**, but we must meet the critics' objections. In the creation of Eve from Adam's cell, the 'Y' chromosome would be removed.
   With the Virgin, it would be added by the Holy Spirit (Lk 1:31–35).
   Verse 31 says it was a conception, therefore not parthenogenesis.
   Holy Spirit would supply or recode DNA for the Word made flesh. Alleles (genetic pairs) from the two sources, human and divine, would become pheno, typically one, for one personality not two natures.
   'With God nothing shall be impossible' (v 37).
   John 1:1–14 applies Genesis 1:1–5.

2. **Near East marriage customs**
   Engagement could not be dissolved without a divorce. Consummation not allowed until marriage.
   This made possible the virgin conception, then marriage and Christ's virgin birth within wedlock.

3. **Kindred tablets of descent**
   Both from the same ancestor by different routes.
   Mary also had a kindred link with a priestly line (Zechariah). For Jesus to be born in Bethlehem, Joseph must also be descended from David.

4. **Salvation** could only be accomplished by a God/Man.

THE DNA CODE AND THE INCARNATION

The Scriptures insist that the Word which was coded in the beginning became recoded in the virgin Mary at the Incarnation by similar agencies as those at the beginning.

The prologue to the fourth Gospel is a striking application of the phraseology of Genesis 1. It becomes very much more arresting today as we are able to reconsider it in the light of our knowledge of genetic coding. 'The Word' of John 1, known to the Greeks as the Logos, is an application of the repeated expression of Genesis, 'God said'. This is emphasised by other analogies which John makes. The passage is among the best known of the Bible:

> In the beginning was the Word
> And the Word was with God,
> And the Word was God.
> The same was in the beginning with God.
> All things were made through him,
> And without him was not anything made that was made.

The prologue concludes with a statement demonstrating to us that this same 'Word' who himself coded all life in the beginning, graciously allowed himself to become coded in the DNA of the Incarnation:

> And the Word became flesh, and dwelt among us,
> And we beheld his glory,
> The glory as of the only begotten of the Father,
> Full of grace and truth.

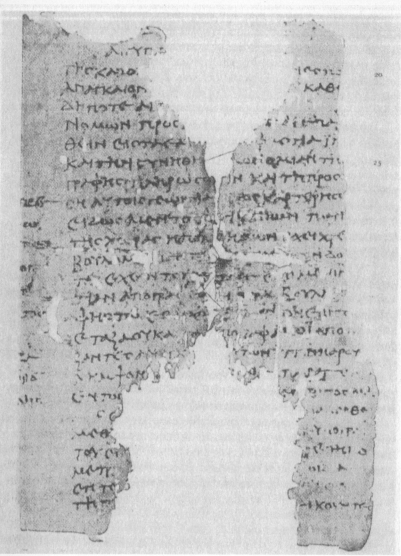

Fig. 21. Census of Caesar. An example of an edict, 2,000 years old, commanding everyone to return to their native town, similar to the one recorded in Luke 2:1–6 which led to Jesus being born in Bethlehem. Some doubted whether a Roman empire would order their people back to their ancestral town. In answer, this papyrus poster was found in the sands of Egypt. The world for 'enrolment' is exactly the same as is used in Luke 2:1–6. Different words could have been used, but this was not the case. *Translation*: Gaius Bivius Maximus, Prefect of Egypt, saith: The enrolment by household being at hand, it is necessary to notify all who for any cause soever are outside their homes to return to their domestic hearths, that they may also accomplish the customary dispensation of enrolment and continue steadfastly in the husbandry that belongeth to them.

Courtesy: British Museum

24   MORE HISTORICAL THAN ANYBODY

I continue to get letters or see in newspapers the assertion that the picture of Jesus in the New Testament is not a factual one. This is often backed up with the assertion that there is little in history about the man Jesus Christ.

Such statements are completely without foundation. They only deceive people who have no knowledge of the facts.

The New Testament story of the Lord Jesus has three times more evidence of its accuracy than there is for any other figure of history; three times more than anything about any of the Roman emperors; and many times more written copies of the original accounts. Compared with any event of history, the New Testament has abundantly more reliable documents than any other.

Professor F.F. Bruce of Manchester University, says that Caesar's *Gallic War* with which many students are familiar, has only nine old copies and the oldest of those is 900 years after Caesar's day, yet nobody questions those. In contrast, the New Testament has 5,000 Greek manuscripts of the New Testament in whole or part. The oldest full copies go back to about AD 330 and part of St John's Gospel which has survived, actually goes back to within a few years of his original writing, and we have fragments of St Mark's Gospel, St James' letter and 1 Timothy, older than AD 68.

Of the works of the Roman historian Livy of Christ's time, only 20 old copies survive. What a contrast to the 5,000 of the New Testament. The well-known Roman historian, Tacitus, has only four surviving old copies of his Annals. What a contrast to the 5,000 old manuscripts of the New Testament.

Concerning the famous history by Herodotus, the oldest copy

of the original is 1,300 years later than when it was written. Professor Bruce comments, 'Yet no classical scholar would listen to an argument that the authenticity of Herodotus was in doubt.'

He then reviews the wealth of evidence we have for the New Testament and shows what a contrast it is to secular history.

CHECKPOINTS

THE REAL JESUS

1. **Motive** of critics is to say that Jesus was only a prophet who, in the second century the Church exaggerated into a miracle-working Messiah.
   Reason: they thought miracles impossible.

2. **Pilate** was said to be fiction, but:
   Memorial stone found at Caesarea barracks.
   Tacitus, Roman historian AD 115, 'Executed by sentence of Pontius Pilate, in reign of Tiberius'.

3. **Jesus more historical than anybody:**
   Three times more evidence than any other historical figure, Caesar's *Gallic Wars* has only nine copies, none older than 900 years after Caesar.
   New Testament has 5,000 Greek manuscripts. Oldest fragment dates before AD 68.
   Tacitus has only four old copies.
   Heroditus history – oldest copy of original is 1,300 years later.

4. **First-century historians refer to Christ:**
   Eight non-Christians: Tacitus, Suetonious, Serapian,

Phlegon, Lucian and Josephus, as well as references by Pliny and Thallus.

Nine antagonists: Talmuds.

Four Gospels: eyewitnesses, 'accurately' (Lk 1:1). Quotations from Apostolic Fathers AD 86–108 from all the New Testament.

5. **Examples:**

Josephus – fairly full concise summary of Christ.

Pliny – in a sacrament Christians 'worship Jesus as a God'.

Thallus – three-hour darkness reached Rome.

Serapion – Fall of Jerusalem because Jews executedJesus.

Talmuds – 'Hanged him on Eve of Passover'. 'Illegitimate.'

25 BULLETIN: A STRANGE INQUEST

Seven high-ranking lawyers have given their verdict. An unusual feature was that the body was missing. Search parties reported that a man had been seen walking seven miles on badly torn and wounded feet.

Three of these lawyers received such reports with *great scepticism*. Their names were Gilbert West, Lord Littleton and Frank Morison. After intensive detective investigation they reached an amazing conclusion. The other four also used their long legal expertise to thoroughly sift such fantastic claims.

The claims were that the missing body had actually chatted with hundreds of people for nearly six weeks all around the country! Had he been really dead? The chief executioner, on solemn oath, said he had thrust a spear right through the victim's heart which entirely emptied itself in blood and serum. All the other witnesses were called, and the unanimous verdict by all these leading lawyers was that this man had actually risen from the dead!

The findings of the last four were as follows:

- Sir Edward Clark, KC: 'Evidence is conclusive'.
- Lord Lyndhurst: 'Such evidence has never broken down.'
- Simon Greenleaf (the great authority on legal procedure): 'No possible motive for fabrication.'
- Professor Anderson: 'Empty tomb stands – a veritable rock of evidence.'

CHECKPOINTS

LAWYERS' INQUEST

1. **Three lawyers** set out to prove Jesus did not rise:
   Frank Morison, *Who Moved the Stone?*
   Gilbert West and Lord Littleton, both Rationalists.
   They examined evidence by legal methods.
   It proved the Resurrection. They set out the evidence.

2. **Two eminent Christian lawyers** give their legal findings:
   Professor Norman Anderson, 'Empty tomb stands, a veritable rock of evidence.'
   Sir Edward Clark K.C. 'Evidence is conclusive.'
   Lord Lyndhurst, 'Such evidence has never broken down.'
   Simon Greenleaf, 'No possible motive for fabrication.'

3. **Dr John Stott** examines the mystery of the empty, hollow, mummy-like grave wrappings. They made John believe when he saw them.

4. **Prophesied in Old Testament**
   Psalm 16:8–11; Psalm 22; Psalm 110:1; Psalm 118:22–24; Job 19:25; Isaiah 53:10.

5. **Jesus predicted** his death and resurrection over seven times:
   Matthew 12:38; 16:21; 17:9; 17:22; 20:18; 26:32; John 2:18.
   But they could not understand it.

6. **When he had risen** (Luke 24:45)
   'He opened their understanding that they might understand the Scriptures, and he said to them, "Thus it is written and thus it behoved Christ to suffer, and to rise from the dead the third day".'

THE RESURRECTION JIGSAW PUZZLE

What excitement and confusion on that first day of the resurrection! There was running about, reporting the empty tomb, seeing angels, seeing Jesus. All this was mixed with incredulity turning into amazed belief. In the confusion of reports coming in, it was not easy to sort out the order of events.

All the accounts from the four Gospels and Paul's list in 1 Corinthians 15, are like a jigsaw puzzle. I have found it fascinating to put the pieces together – and I want to tell you this yes they all fit! Yes, there is harmony in the accounts.

There are 16 jigsaw pieces to the complete picture. They are 16 accounts of 12 incidents. It is because some have reduced the pieces to only half the number that they could not fit them together.

A packed refresher course

Thirty-nine days were to follow in which Jesus appeared and disappeared – five-and-a-half weeks in which they never knew when he might appear again, when he would appear to give them further instructions and insights into the Scriptures and an understanding of the purposes of God for the world. Nearly six weeks in which their own hearts were to be examined, in which they were to see their weaknesses and be prepared for the Lord's new miraculous strength.

CHECKPOINTS

RESURRECTION JIGSAW PUZZLE
Fitting in twelve appearances of the Risen Jesus.

1. **Jesus appeared five times on the first Resurrection Day**
   Two women saw the stone rolled away, Mary Magdalene and
   Mary, James' mother. 'Men will only think it's a tale.' They
   told no one, only 'Body is missing'.
   • Mary Magdalene stays and sees Jesus.
   • Mary catches up with former Mary and both see Jesus.
   • Christ's personal interview with guilty Peter.
   • Two walking to Emmaus. Tell apostles, who exclaim, 'He's
     appeared to Peter.'
   • Sunday evening to all in the upper room. They had been
     prepared by reports. 'I'm not a ghost!' Old Testament fore-
     told it all.

2. **Next 39 days, another seven times**
   (A packed refresher course on Old Testament prophecies)
   • Next Sunday in the upper room to all, especially Thomas
     (Jn 20:26–31).
   • At Galilee lakeside as reminded by the angel. Seven disci-
     ples including John (Jn 21:1–14).
   • On a mountain in Galilee to all eleven apostles. Recom-
     missioning (Mt 28:16).
   • One hundred and twenty including Holy Family and holy
     women in upper room (Ac 1).
   • Five hundred brethren in one gathering (1 Cor 15:6).
   • Then to James, half-brother of Jesus – Christ's origin need-
     ed explaining (1 Cor 15:7).
   • The Ascension from Mount of Olives with promise to
     return (Lk 24:44–49; Ac 1:3–8).

26 THE DEAD SEA SCROLLS

Unfortunately, the media is often ready to seize on statements by a sensationalist if they knock the Church or the Bible.

There have been several instances of this concerning the Dead Sea Scrolls. It has given the public the impression that they expose Christianity as something invented by those who wrote the scrolls from 130 BC to AD 68 and they go on to accuse the Church of trying to cover up these things. The accusation is laughable for anyone who knows even a few basic facts. The Scrolls actually are a great testimony to the accuracy of our Bible text.

Instead of there being an attempt to prevent the scrolls coming to public attention, it was prominent clerics and scholars of the Church who rescued many copies and bought them so that they could be translated for all to read.

NO COVER-UP

Five of the Scrolls were found in cave one. The Archbishop of the Syrian Orthodox monastery in Jerusalem bought them and, as he could not read Hebrew, he told the American School of Oriental Research about the find, hoping that their scholars could translate the Scrolls, so there was no cover-up there.

By the Lord's providence, John Trevor was director and he was also a good photographer. He photographed each column of the great scroll of Isaiah. This was 24 feet long and ten inches high. In great excitement, he sent some of the prints to Dr W.F. Albright in the USA.

Albright replied immediately.

'My heartiest congratulations on the greatest manuscript discovery of modern times . . . What an incredible find! And there

can happily not be the slightest doubt in the world about the gen-
uineness of the manuscript . . . I date it around 100 BC.' He
meant that it was about that year that this copy was made from
earlier copies. These in turn went back to when Isaiah wrote the
original during a period around 740 to 722 BC.

CHECKPOINTS

A COVER-UP?

1. **There was not a cover-up** by the Church. Clerics and schol-
   ars rescued the Scrolls, e.g.:
   Syrian Orthodox Archbishop.
   American Oriental School of Research.
   John Trevor sent photo of Isaiah to Dr W.F. Albright.
   Professor Sukenik bought three scrolls for University of
   Jerusalem the day on which the UNO created the State of
   Israel.
   Yigel Yadin significance, son of Professor Sukenik.
   Yigil Yadin quotes 'Assumption of Moses' which instructs
   scroll preservation. Also Jeremiah 32:14.

   Eleven caves 200 manuscripts covering every book except
   Esther.
   + Essene commentaries.
   Essenes described by Origen AD 185–254.

2. **Cover-up was by sceptics**
   They misrepresented them before they had been read.
   Later challenged by Yadin, Vermes and Carpenter.
   Fourteen years later another critic confessed to sensational
   inaccuracy.
   Geza, Vermes and Albright correct false statements of others
   as 'emotive' and say 'not affected Bible message'. Supported
   accuracy of copying.

Millar Burrows agrees.

Demolishes 'second' Isaiah theory. God proves he is God by foretelling Cyrus and Exile. Josephus agrees. Then, an Australian writer in 1992 probably misinterprets Hosea's experiences as reference to Christ.

3. **Essenes** did not invent Christ, neither did Jesus get his ideas from them.

They were quoting Old Testament prophecies describing Christ, e.g.:

'The Son of Man' (Dan 7:13).

'Teacher of Righteousness' (Deut 18:15–19) etc.

'He is to judge the world and save elect and divide between sons of darkness and sons of light' (Dan 12:2,1 and Joel, Isaiah, Ezekiel and Zechariah).

'The New Covenant' (Jer 31:31–34).

THE SCROLL OF ISAIAH

Those of us who have seen the Isaiah scroll know that what is now chapter 39 in our Bible ends one line up from the bottom of the scroll column. The next line at the very bottom starts what is now our chapter 40, which some thought was by a different author, but obviously if another author was writing, a fresh column would have been started.

As I have said, it demolishes the theory of two Isaiahs. If you look at the photo of the end of our chapter 39, you will see that it ends one line up from the bottom and what we now call chapter 40 starts on the bottom line and continues onto the next column. There is obviously no concept of an ending and starting of a new work by someone else.

The critics denied that it could be one work as early as 722 BC because they did not believe that there was a God who could reveal his future plans. They quote those passages in Isaiah which speak of Judah's return from Babylon through the help from Cyrus the Persian Emperor.

Fig 22. Scroll of Isaiah. This scroll was found by a goat-herd boy and sold for one shilling (5 pence). It was later purchased for £20,000. It proved that all our modern copies are faithful and accurate copies of the original by Isaiah. It also confirms that the 66 chapters of Isaiah were written by one author, namely Isaiah himself. This scroll would have been copied from an original copy around 150–200 BC.

CHECKPOINTS

USEFUL LIST OF EVIDENCE

1. Scrolls prove the accuracy with which our Scriptures have been copied and handed down. They were copied for over 1,000 years without an intervening copy surviving until the Dead Sea Scrolls were found.

2. They support claims of the Massorete method to ensure accurate copying.

3. Sir Frederick Kenyon, former Director of the British Museum, says that Bible copies are three times more reliable that the secular classics such as Shakespeare, Marlowe or Greek and Roman history which nobody bothers to question.

4. A fragment of St James' epistle was found in cave seven. This must have been copied from James' original some years before the jars were sealed in AD 68; this cave also gave the fragment from Mark's Gospel.

5. The Scrolls support the assertion that Isaiah was written by the **one** prophet Isaiah in about 740 BC, showing that God **did** foretell his future plans. 'I am God and there is no-one else . . . declaring the end from the beginning, and from ancient times the things that are not yet done . . . I will fulfil all my purpose' (Is 46:9–10).

6. The Scrolls got their anticipation of Christian phrases from the prophecies of the Old Testament:
   • 'New Covenant' from Jeremiah 31:31, 500 years earlier;
   • 'Son of Man' from Daniel 7:13 about 500 years earlier;
   • 'The 'Righteous Teacher' who would judge the world from Deuteronomy 18:15–19 (1400 BC) and Isaiah 42:14 (750 BC) and other prophecies;
   • 'Bread and wine' – Genesis 14:18 and Psalm 110:4.

7. The three sections of Old Testament Scripture are summed up as complete, just as Jesus named them in Luke 24:44, i.e. the Torah, the Prophets and the Psalms, which all foretold the Messiah Jesus.

27 THE OMINOUS YEAR OF AD 66

Cestius surrounded Jerusalem for five days and his troops battered at the walls. Even the Christians in the city were apprehensive. Had not Luke recorded the words of Jesus years earlier, thirteen years ago in AD 53? It warned the Christians to evacuate Jerusalem when armies surrounded it. (Matthew and Mark had not recorded the bit about the armies.) What did it mean? How could they escape if armies were all around the walls?

The deep valleys around the east, south and west of Jerusalem made the walls impossible to attack, so Cestius attacked from the north. The Christians wondered even more how they could obey Christ and escape.

Josephus then adds these significant words: 'He [General Cestius] retired from the city, without any reason in the world.'

But there was a reason! Can you guess it? Jesus had prophesied to the believers, 'When you see Jerusalem surrounded by armies, then know that its destruction is near. Then let those who are in Judea fly to the mountains, and let those who are inside the city depart, and let not those who are out in the country enter the city.' This particular warning was only recorded by Luke.

Josephus says, 'The Jews, after they had beaten General Cestius, were greatly encouraged by their unexpected success.' But he says, 'After this calamity had befallen General Cestius, many of the most eminent of the Jews swam away from the city as if from a ship when it was going to sink.' Who were these people?

It is Hegessippus, another historian, who tells us that those who forsook the city were the Christians. They read an oracle left by Christ. Now what oracle was that? It was recorded only in

Luke's Gospel. Here is evidence that Luke wrote well before AD 66. Indeed, Luke's Gospel had been written thirteen years earlier.

CHECKPOINTS

JOSEPHUS' HISTORY

1. **Jewish non-Christian** wrote history for Romans as observer.
   His record showed how Christ's prophecies were fulfilled AD 66–70.
   High priest Ananias executed James when Festus died. Festus also features in Acts 25 and 26.
   King Agrippa and Queen Bernice in Acts also figure in history.
   Florus slew 3,600 Jewish worshippers to steal treasure: this sparked revolt.
   Mob massacred Roman garrison and took their war machines.

2. **Cestius** surrounded Jerusalem in AD 66. Josephus said certain ones fled.
   Luke recorded this 13 years earlier (21:20,21) as the sign to flee whole country.
   Jesus knew this would start three-and-a-half years' war over the whole land.
   Bethsaida, Chorazim, Capernaum would suffer. 'Woe unto you,' wrote Capernaum's converted tax collector (Mt 11:20–23).

3. **Vespasian and Titus** in winter of AD 69 prepare attack on Jerusalem.
   'Pray that your flight be not in winter.'
   Campaign postponed. Nero had died.
   Rebels, Zealots, and temple guard renewed in-fighting.

4. **Titus** marched up as Passover approached.
   Sacrilege committed by Zealots warned remaining Christians.
   Jesus had wept 'Your enemies will make a bank and hem you in.'
   Three million Jews were trapped.
   Sacrifices ceased for ever as Daniel 9:27 prophesied.
   None necessary after Christ's sacrifice (Heb 10:1–22).

5. **'Captives into all nations'** Luke 21:24.
   Titus sent best young men for march of triumph. Now depicted on Rome's ancient Arch of Triumph with the branched lampstand of Exodus 25.
   Seventeen-year-olds sent in chains to Egyptian mines. Under seventeen-year-olds sold as slaves around the empire.

6. **'Until Gentile rule ends in Jerusalem'** Luke 21.
   It ended in 1967 with Israel back in Jerusalem city.

ACTS VINDICATED BY ARCHAEOLOGY

Sir William Ramsay was one who started by assuming that Acts was written too late to be accurate, but his archaeological discoveries and his knowledge of Roman history compelled him to revise his opinion. This was partly because the detailed descriptions and titles of the officials Paul met in various provinces were completely accurate. This knowledge of Luke who wrote the Acts must have been contemporary with the events because the titles of the provincial governors changed suddenly at times if the status of provinces changed. Yet Luke always uses the correct title of which there are about eleven occurrences.

Clues to dates of writing

Professor F.F. Bruce of Manchester University has pointed out that a clue to the date of the completion of St Luke's Gospel is the date of the end of Acts which is a sequel to it. It is obvious that Acts ends unfinished. It was written up-to-date. Paul was a prisoner in Rome awaiting trial before Nero. If it had been written after that trial in AD 62, Luke would surely have recorded it. We can safely conclude then, that Acts was written before AD 62 and Luke's Gospel a reasonable time before that.

What testimony have we to Matthew and Mark? A Christian writing as early as AD 100 was a disciple of St John. His name is Papias, and concerning Mark's Gospel, Papias says that Mark was Peter's companion and 'wrote down accurately all that Peter mentioned, whether sayings or doings of Christ . . . for he paid attention to this one thing, not to omit anything that he heard, nor to include any false statements.'

Of Matthew's Gospel, Papias said in AD 100, 'Matthew compiled the sayings in the Hebrew Aramaic tongue (the language of Jesus) and everyone translated them as best he could.' Now it is significant that it is in Matthew's Gospel that we have the longest sections of 'sayings' of Jesus.

While he was a Roman tax collector he would send reports of the taxes taken down in shorthand. Jesus therefore selected him as he would follow him with his note board to jot down Christ's sayings in shorthand. Disciples of rabbis at that time were a small group recruited to recall the teaching of their rabbi in this way.

ST MATTHEW'S SHORTHAND

In 1997 a shorthand test was discovered on writing materials in a Roman office at Vindolanda, dated AD 97. Three or four fragments had been written in shorthand. This was proof that the government in Rome made use of shorthand and army scribes were expected to make their reports in it. It is now known that their income tax officers also sent their reports to Rome in shorthand. this would be why Jesus chose Matthew, the Roman tax collector, to follow him so that he could write down quickly his teaching as he was giving it. Not enough survives yet for modern scholars to be able to crack the code but a sample is given opposite.

I have given you evidence to help your faith in God's remarkable book. Paul wrote, 'We overthrow all reasonings and every proud thing that exalts itself against the knowledge of God and take captive every theory to the obedience of Christ' (2 Cor 10:5).

In the first Bible I bought after my conversion, I wrote in the flyleaf (prophetically?):

We've travelled together, my Bible and I,
Through all kinds of weather, with smile and with sigh.
In sorrow or sunshine, in tempest or calm,
Thy friendship unchanging, my lamp and my psalm.

So now who shall part us, my Bible and I,
Shall 'isms' or 'schisms' or 'new lights', who try?
Shall shadow or substance, or stone for good bread,
Supplant thy sound wisdom, give folly instead?

Oh no, my dear Bible, exponent of light,
Thou sword of the Spirit, put error to flight.
And still through life's journey, until my last sigh,
We'll travel together, my Bible and I.

(author unknown)

Fig. 23. Roman Vindolanda writing tablets in shorthand text AD 97 discovered in 1997. Shorthand text possibly upside down!

28 THAT AMAZING BOOK

The Bible is the most remarkable book in the world, looked at from any angle. It is the oldest book in the world; it has survived down 40 centuries of human history. Other ancient records have perished and have only been discovered by archaeology, but the Bible as a book has been handed down the ages.

Why is this? It is because believers were told by God that its records were to lead to the Saviour of the world, that it must be preserved and handed down from Abraham to the Apostles and from Adam to the second Adam.

The first section of holy Scripture was the Torah of Moses from Genesis to Deuteronomy, then to this, God gave the prophets ever-increasing information to add. When the prophesied picture of the precious Saviour was complete in the Old Testament, the world waited 400 years until, 'In the fulfilment of time, God sent his Son'.

The living witnesses of Christ then wrote the New Testament. The canon of Scripture closed when the last witness died.

Because holy and honest men were inspired by the Holy Spirit (to use St Peter's words), those records were accurate and affirmed by many infallible proofs (to use Luke's words).

FIRST AMONG NATIONS

The Bible is also remarkable because it has been the first book to be put into writing for a high percentage of nations, and has been the foundation of their civilisation. When it has been neglected or disbelieved, that country has declined, as God said it would.

CHECKPOINTS

THAT AMAZING BOOK

1. **Oldest book in the world:**
   4,000 years to Abraham; 3,400 years to Moses.
   Why? To prepare for Saviour (Gen 12).
   Prophecy ceased 400 BC to wait for Saviour.
   Other countries' histories discovered only by archaeology.

2. **Miraculous preservation:**
   Attempts to destroy it and Christians.
   John for 'Word of God' on Isle of Patmos.
   Rome until 4th century. Traitors.
   Medieval church banned it because it exposed added errors.
   More subtle Rationalists by Criticism infiltrating the churches.
   Satan says prophecies are fraudulent but Satan is the big fraud.
   John 8:44, Revelation 12:9.

3. **Says how God inspired the prophets:**
   - By audible dictation (not by divination – forbidden, Lev 19:31; Deut 18:10–20).
     Moses: audibly and face to face (Num 12). 'I speak to Moses mouth to mouth and visibly.' Two-thirds of Exodus, Leviticus and Numbers are written down as dictated.
     Isaiah: 'I heard the voice of the LORD'.
     Ezekiel: 'Hear with your ears'.
     Daniel: 'He talked with me.' 'I heard but did not understand'.
     (So it was not his own ideas.)
   - By vision usually with voice.
   - Told to write it down.
     'Write on a tablet and note in a book' (Is 8:1).
     'Write all the words I have spoken in a book' (Jer 36:2, RSV).

'Write . . . I the LORD have spoken it. It will come to pass' (Ezek 24:2,3,14).
'Write the vision, make it plain' (Hab 2:2,3, RSV).

4. **For all time:**
'Heaven and earth will pass away but my words will never pass away,' said Jesus in all Synoptics (Mk 13:31).
'Your Word is forever' (Ps 119:89), 'Endures for ever' (1 Pet), 'Not one comma [*yod*] will fail,' said Jesus. 'Any teacher teaching it will be called least' (Mt 5:18,19).

5. **Scriptures claim:**
'All scripture is given by inspiration of God' (2 Tim 3:16).
'Holy men spake as they were borne along by the Spirit of God' (2 Pet 1:21).
'David spoke by the Holy Spirit,' said Jesus (Mk 12:36).
'The scripture cannot be broken' (Jn 10:35).
'Thy Word is truth' (Jn 17:17).
'Anyone adding or taking away from this book will have his place in the Holy City removed,' said God (Rev 22:19).

TAX AND SHORTHAND

As a trained tax collector of Rome, Matthew would continue his customary habit of taking down notes in the vernacular 'of all that Jesus began to do and to teach'. According to the Early Fathers, this was in Aramaic, the very language Jesus used.

Normally, when making tax reports, Matthew would then translate his notes into Greek and send them to Rome. It would, therefore, be natural for him to translate his own notes taken during Christ's ministry into Greek after Pentecost when 'this gospel was to be preached in all the world' (Mt 26:13).

The Early Fathers date it eight or ten years after the resurrection. This would be during the expansion beyond Samaria into the Greek world; Matthew would see the necessity as indicated in Matthew 28:19,20, 'Go therefore and make disciples in all nations . . . teaching them to observe all things whatever I gave to you in command.'

It comes as a surprise to learn from Roman records that Matthew would be taking it all down in shorthand – a tax collector's shorthand script, then he would rewrite it in the vernacular (Aramaic), then translate it into a Greek report to Rome. Is that why we get the fullest records of Christ's brilliant preaching from Matthew.

Rome had a very elaborate and detailed tax system so that no one would escape. There were 111 categories of tax. As a tax collector Levi (an appropriate name before he became a disciple) would have full particulars – long before he became Matthew – of every household.

CHECKPOINTS

THE BIBLE SPEAKS

Testimony of early writers AD 70–170

1. **Matthew** AD 30. Aramaic notes made during ministry. Papias born AD 70.
   Aramaic underlies Greek translation – Bruce, Chilton, Howard.
   Note-taking was prevalent custom in Christ's time.
   'Certain Matthew passages more original than Mark's' (Blomberg).

2. **Mark** St Peter's. Probably written in Rome AD 44 after Peter's escape (Ac 12).
   'Wrote down accurately . . . paid attention not to include any false statement' Papias.

3. **Luke** AD 54 or 57. Sir William Ramsey's archaeological research finds Luke very accurate. Luke gives his methods:
   • Information obtained from eyewitnesses
   • Complete understanding from the first
   • Wrote an order of events
   • Others he knew had written their experiences
   • Infallible proofs of Christ's life and miracles.

4. **Acts** Completed AD 62 before Nero outcome was known, therefore Luke was earlier, probably AD 54 (2 Cor 8:18) or during Paul's first imprisonment AD 57. Cf. Acts 21:8,9.

5. **John** says:
   • He was an eyewitness (19:35)
   • He confirms truth and accuracy
   • He was the closest companion to Jesus (21:20–24)
   • John's Gospel supplementary to Synoptics but before 'Wars of Jews'. Therefore AD 65 (J. Robinson).

6. **Other:**
  - Significance of prophecy of Fall of Jerusalem
  - Warnings useless if written afterwards
  - Luke warned of armies surrounding Jerusalem AD 66 Matthew and Mark warned of Fall in AD 70
  - James, half brother of Jesus, very significant as Josephus refers to him.

In answer to accusations that Luke had inaccuracies, Sir William Ramsey travelled around the Mediterranean researching the history of St Luke's time. He then wrote his famous book, *St Paul Roman Citizen and Traveller*, in which he showed that he found every historical and political detail fully accurate in St Luke's works. Agnostics still ignore his findings.

29 THE PREPLANNED DESTINY OF LIFE

In comparing religions the question is often asked, 'What is special about Jesus?' The most effective reply is that which Jesus himself used and became the method adopted by the disciples afterwards. He showed that God had foretold and prepared for Jesus Christ for at least 2,000 years before he came. No other founder of a religion claims this. The prophesied details of his first coming are amazing, and are all fulfilled.

Q   *What of his prophesied second coming? Are we to take that seriously?*

This is a relevant question because in many circles it has become the fashion to avoid recognising the signs. Various excuses are given. Some have burnt their fingers they say, yet concerning other important doctrines there have always been people who lacked wisdom in their statements yet the Scripture teaching has not been abandoned on those issues.

What did Jesus mean when he said, 'When you see these things coming to pass, then know that my coming is near'? Did he intend that Christians living near that time should recognise the signs, and perhaps have extra means of doing so?

Some Christians have found that the wise application of these signs has been an effective means of arousing the interest of the indifferent. Many statements by Christ show that he intended us to recognise and use the signs unfolding all about us.

You can see why some false teaching makes some Christians weak in their witness to a sceptical world. Concerning science, the Old Testament is treated as a book of myths; concerning archaeology, the student is fed on wrong dating – not the Bible dates; concerning prophecy, he is told that the New Testament church expected Christ to return in their own life-time. Consequently, such students see no remarkable Creator's knowledge displayed in the Bible; they dismiss the harmony between archaeological tablets and Bible history, and see no significance in the signs of Christ's near return which are happening all around us.

I have given you convincing evidence to use in *Evidence for Truth: Science, Volume 1*; also amazing archaeological correlation which confronts the critics in *Volume 2*; so now we ask what are those prophetic signs, and are there indications in Scripture that Christ knew that his return would be after a long time?

In answer to that last question, I bring to your notice areas of information which have long been neglected and even forgotten.

The evidence of prophecy, however, not only concerns Christ's second coming, it also establishes the claims of Christ made at his first coming. This is the effective answer to those who contend that Christ was only one of many prophets and only one founder among other religions.

Concerning scriptures which show that the period between the two comings would be a long one, a brief summary first will help you to see the relevance of the actual signs of his coming.

Briefly, God's time schedule in a number of scriptures is that Israel's scattering among the nations would last 2,500 years. This is revealed to Moses, Hosea, Daniel and Peter. The re-establishment of Israel on the map of Palestine after this period is a prelude to Christ's return. Old faithful scholars' works on this have been neglected. Also, Christ gave many indications that his return would be after a long period of time. The evidence for all this was to be given later but, after having voiced those points, the signs are then seen to be absolutely relevant. In the following chapters I outline the signs for your use.

30 EFFECTIVE EVIDENCE

Whom are we to believe? Was Jesus Christ all that he claimed to be? Is he just one among other founders of religion?

Prophecies in the Old Testament are an effective insight. No other founder of religion was foretold in the way that God prepared the world for the first coming of Jesus Christ 2,000 years ago. Every aspect of Christ's birth, life, atoning death and resurrection were described to the prophets hundreds of years before he came. From 2,000 years *before* Christ, the full identity and credentials of the Messiah were described.

In order to help you master these, I give you full coverage for your own effectiveness. It was Christ's method and it became the apostles' method to demonstrate that Christ was in all the Old Testament Scriptures.

There are also just as many prophecies describing his second coming and the signs which would show that it was near. These are effective in revealing to friends that the Bible message is relevant. Indeed, as you study the information you will find that it is an amazing eye-opener to the significance of what is happening in the world today. It is very topical and easy to converse about. Many an indifferent person has been sparked to eager desire for more insight. People generally are not aware of the amazing details in those prophecies. It is extraordinary how even commentaries on the Bible seem to miss the thrust of many a book of the prophets. Why is this?

I shall bring out all such evidence for your use. Without understanding this, the Church is weakened in making its message relevant and convincing.

CHECKPOINTS

PROPHETIC EVIDENCE

Two benefits of evidence from prophecy
1. For Christ's first coming it proves his claims, prophesied by many prophets.
2. For Christ's second coming, it is topical and makes the Bible relevant for non-Christians today. They see that events prophesied are daily world news.

Fashionable fallacies which blunt perception
1. *That disciples expected Christ's return in their lifetime.*
   Reply:
   a) They were intended to do so that their hopes were kept alive.
   b) **Enigmatic metaphors** intended to keep expectancy alive.
      - e.g. Mark 9:1–2 says they will not die until the Kingdom comes with power. Next verse shows the Transfiguration as a fulfilment and Luke 9:28 connects the two. Power came to the spiritual kingdom at Pentecost.
      - John 21:21–23. John corrects wrong impression in v 23.
   c) **'Certain things.'** Jesus did not know the actual date (Mk 13:32) but he knew it would be after a long time: 'These things must first be fulfilled but the end is not yet . . . Gospel first to all nations' (Mt 24:4).
   d) **What things?**
      - Fall of Jerusalem AD 70, scattering of Jews (Lk 21:24) rise of Mohamet (Mt 24:24). The return of Israel after 2,520 years from 603 BC.
      - Matthew 25:5. Coming delayed so the Church falls asleep (v 48). Luke 19:12 'Far country'
      - Two thousand year-days Hosea 5:15; 6:2; 2 Peter 3:8; 2 Thessalonians 2:3 falling away first.
      - 2,500 years to pass. See item c.

2. *That God abandoned Israel in favour of the Church.*
Reply:
Romans 11:24, Israel to be grafted back in. Leviticus 26:44, Jeremiah 33:24–26.

3. *That Israel's return refers to end of 70 years exile.*
Reply:
From exile only 2 tribes returned in 506 BC (Ez 2:1; 4:1). From the diaspora all tribes are to return in the 20th century AD after 2,520 years. See p.206. (Is 11:12; Ezek 37:16–24; Hos 1:10, 11; Dan 12:7).

31 SIGNS

A lady once remarked to me, 'Isn't it tragic that we hear little about the second coming just now when the signs show that it is near?' Yes, there are so many unmistakable signs. It is an impressive list which is powerful for convincing the casual enquirer.

'When you see these signs,' said the Lord Jesus Christ, 'know that my return is near.'

So let us take the word 'signs' as an acrostic to use when discussing them with a friend.

S for Science; I for Israel; G for Gospel; N for Nations; S for Society.

Many scriptures speak of stress, vandalism, terrorism, lawlessness and the increase of wickedness which would characterise 'the last days'. 2 Timothy 3:1–6 reads like a daily press report. In fact, when one man in prison heard the passage read out, he asked, 'What paper was that in?'

In the last days there will come times of stress, for people will be lovers of self, lovers of money, proud, arrogant, blasphemous, disobedient to their parents, ungrateful, unholy, cruel, refusing reconciliation, slanderers, sexual libertines, fierce, haters of good, treacherous, reckless, swollen with conceit, lovers of pleasure rather than lovers of God, holding a form of religion but denying its power. Avoid such people.

This prophecy then moves on to the feature of increased education which does not promote God's revealed truth.

They will be for ever learning but can never arrive at the truth . . . opposing the truth, men of corrupt minds and counterfeit faith . . . evil imposters, from bad to worse, deceivers and being deceived . . . people will not endure sound teaching . . . teachers will turn it into myths.

Certainly this prophecy is relevant. It is this unbelief and perverting of the truth which is the cause of our social ills today. Young people are not given guidance from divine authority which promises, 'Do these things and you will prosper in a good and happy life'.

Social geography also illustrates another prophecy. Students learn that the first invention to make the boys visit the lasses in the farther village was the boneshaker bicycle, and then the motorcar for the select few. Now, aeroplanes carrying 400 at a time speed through the air all over the world.

'Science and travel shall greatly increase.' That is what God told Daniel in chapter 12 verse 4. Every time you pass a travel shop, you can say to your friend 'Daniel 12:4!' Every time an airliner flies over your head, you can point up and say, 'Daniel 12:4.'

CHECKPOINTS

AN ACROSTIC

'When you see these signs, know that my return is near'

S for Science
Knowledge of travel increased (Dan 12:4).
Ever learning but erroneous (2 Tim 3:7).
Strong delusion to believe evolution (2 Thess 2:8–11).
Air travel from afar (Is 60:8,9).
As birds flying (Is 31:5).
Nuclear fission (Mk 13:25; 2 Pet 3:12).

I for Israel
The re-united ten and two tribes will return in the last days as
Israel (Is 11:10–16; Jer 16:14–16).
After a long time without a country (Hos 1:10,11; 3:4,5; Ezek
37:20–28; Amos 9:9–15). Israel was granted a home in 1917.
Moslem date 1335 = AD 1917 (Joel 3:1,2; Dan 12:11,12).
Nailprints to convert Israel (Rom 11:25,26; Zech 12:10).

G for Gospel
All nations must hear as a witness (Mt 24:14).
The ionosphere is in mid-heaven for radio waves and gospel
proclamation (Rev 14:6).
Mouth of unclean propaganda war by Satan (Rev 16:13).
Christian radio penetrates closed countries (Rom 10:17,18).

N for Nations
Old Roman Empire now European Sovereign states before
Christ descends to rule: (Dan 2:28–45; Rev 13:17,18).
United Nations flag regulates Israel's return; Gentile nations
ruled Jerusalem until 1967 (Lk 21:24,25; Is 11:10–16).
World Wars (Mt 24:6,7).

Natural Signs
Increase in earthquakes, famines, diseases (Mt 24:8).

S for Society
Stress, vandalism, terrorism, lawlessness (2 Tim 3:1–6).
Truth forsaken by teachers (2 Tim 4:3,4).
Occult dabbling increase (1 Tim 4:1,2).
Lawlessness (2 Thess 2:7–9).
Wickedness increases (Lk 21:34–36; Dan 12:10)
Wickedness decreases love of truth (Mt 24:9–13).
Fears and phobias at societies' unrest (Lk 21:26–32).

Now mark the texts in your Bible so that you can use them easily.

32 CHRIST'S CLAIMS

What religion are we to follow? What sect are we to believe? Which founder of religion is the right one? These are the questions confronting you today. There is one sure answer. It is this. Only Jesus Christ was prepared for by prophecies all down the centuries before he came. Only Jesus was prepared for by God. The Creator told all the prophets of his plans to send Jesus to be the Saviour of the world. As the centuries passed by, more and more information was told to holy men who wrote it down in the books of the Old Testament – all the details about the Messiah's divine origin, his virgin conception, his ministry, crucifixion, resurrection, ascension and second coming.

That is why the risen Christ was able to show to his astonished disciples that he was foretold in all the Scriptures from Moses to Malachi. All those 39 books of the Old Testament spoke of Jesus Christ long before he came.

Jesus said to them, 'O foolish men, and slow of heart to believe all that the prophets have written . . .' And beginning with Moses, and all the prophets, he showed to them in all the scriptures the things concerning himself. (Lk 24:25)

Later he reinforced this evidence to all the disciples:

'Everything written about me in the Torah of Moses, and the prophets and the psalms must be fulfilled.' Then he opened their minds to understand the scriptures and he said to them, 'Thus it is written and thus it was necessary for Christ to suffer and rise from the dead the third day, and that repentance and forgiveness of sins should be preached in his name among all nations.'

The disciples and early Christians followed Christ's example of proving him from the prophets and it is your most effective tool as well. That is why we shall look at those prophecies together and find how astonishingly detailed those prophecies were of every aspect of the Lord.

CHECKPOINTS

OLD TESTAMENT PROPHECIES
PROVE CHRIST'S CLAIMS

In all three sections of the Old Testament Christ is described
i.e. in Pentateuch, Prophets and Psalms (Lk 24:25,44)

1. *'Moses wrote of Me'*
   Unleavened Shewbread i.e. sinless, Ex 25:30 (2nd person of Trinity).
   Lamb without blemish (Lev 23:12; 1 Pet 1:18,19).
   A new covenant (Deut 18:15–19).

2. *Prophets also wrote of Jesus*
   To be born in Bethlehem (Mic 5:2).
   As refugee from Egypt (Hos 11:1).
   Ministry to be launched from Galilee (Is 9:1,2).
   Christ's life, death, atonement and resurrection (Is 53).

3. *Psalms* e.g. Psalm 22
   'Pierced hands and feet' and gambling for garments, could not be referring to David.
   See also summaries later in this section.

4. *Divinity described* 'From eternity' (Mic 5:2).
   Son given is part of Holy Trinity (Is 9:6; 7:14; cf. Jn 14:9)

5. *Creating Word*
   'I am the first and the last' (Is 48:12; Rev 1:11; 22:13)
   The Word, God said (Gen 1, Ps 33:6,9).
   'In the beginning The Word' (Jn 1:1)

6. *By virgin conception*
   Genetically through mothers – Eve to Mary. Mitochondrial DNA.
   Mothers only mentioned in David's Kings e.g. 2 Kgs 18:1
   Sonship, Divine source: proud Father (Ps 2:7) 'You are my son.'
   In Gospels, God speaks three times 'You are my beloved son' Matthew 22:42–46. Psalm 110 'LORD said to my Lord'
   Sonship's human source: Body prepared (Ps 40:6–8; cf. Heb. 10:5).
   Branch of royal tree. (Is 6:13; 11:1; 53:2). Shoot out of root. Zechariah 3:8,9. Atones on one day. 6:12,13. Priest-King. (Mary's lineage had priest affinities as well as royal.)
   Hebrew word '*almah*' (Is 7:14) means virgin as in Genesis 24:43 so does '*Parthenos*' in the Greek CT translation and 2 Corinthians 11:2.
   The virgin birth will be long after the exile (Is 6:11–13; 7:8).
   Two geno-type sources become phenotypically one person.

YEAR-DAY PROPHECY

Concerning prophecy, there is a neglected area which is very effective in convincing the unconcerned. Many Christians do not even know about it. Yet God gave it as a special proof of truth for those living 'at the time of end' (Dan 12:9,10). Neglected Bible-believing scholars were Dr Adam Clark, Dr Gratton-Guinness and Dr Basil Atkinson. The witness of Christians would be greatly strengthened again by getting to know about their findings. It is called chronological prophecy.

God told Daniel that the believers living in the end times

would understand something which was concealed even from Daniel. What is it which God wants us to know which is special for those living in the end times?

Daniel asked, 'When shall these things end?' He asked about times and seasons. It wasn't good for him to know. We can see that it would have been discouraging for him to know that the glorious climax to God's plan was still 2,500 years off. So he is given a mysterious number and figures which he didn't understand. Those living in the last days will understand, God said. To Daniel it was sealed up, but in Revelation 22 it is unsealed for those living when the second coming of Christ is near. 'Behold I come quickly,' said Jesus. 'Do not seal up the meaning of these words.'

If the Lord made special provision for us to understand, it is surely wrong to ignore what he intends for the believer today. This is not to be avoided merely because some have misused these figures. Some foolishly predicted the date of the Lord's coming. Those who did were disobedient to Christ's words. 'The day and the hour no-one knows', but observe the signs.

In the Checkpoints on the next page you will see that chronological prophecy was given early in the Bible to Moses as well as later to Daniel.

A dominant feature throughout Scripture is that God is the God of the ages and has pre-planned history. This important theme is neglected but is an important answer to questions on the present evils and purpose unfolding in history.

Agnosticism has invaded theology so that statements like Isaiah 46:9–11 are ignored.

'I am God, and there is none other . . . declaring the end from the beginning and from ancient times things not yet done . . . I have purposed and I will do it.'

To give an insight into the breadth of God's plan, is the purpose of chronological prophecy. Not so much to give dates as to show eras such as 1,260 years and 2,500 years.

CHECKPOINTS

WORLD HISTORY FORETOLD

A **Messiah** to come through Isaac (Gen 17), through Judah (Gen 49:10), succeeding Moses (Deut 18:15), through David (2 Sam 7:16), through Zerubbabel (Zech 4:7), through Mary (Lk 3:27).

B **The order of events** given to Joel, Ezekiel, Daniel and Zechariah:
1) Israel will return in the latter days.
2) When Israel is settled they will be invaded.
3) The Lord will descend to judge the nations.
4) The Lord will then rule over all the earth.
Note the order of events. The New Testament agrees with this order (e.g. Mt 25:31,32; 1 Cor 15:23–28; Rev 19–20).

C **Prophetic time span**: The seven Times or 2,500 years of dispersion of Israel among the nations. One Time = 360 Years.
1) 360 degrees come from Sumerian time unit of 360 (Lev 26:18,21,24,28).
2) Each day represents a year (Num 14:34, Ezek 4:6, Lk 13:32, 33, Dan 9:26).
   Therefore $360 \times 7 = 2{,}520$ years.
   Daniel 12:6,1,260 $\times$ 2 = 2,520.
   First capture of Jerusalem 603 BC to AD 1917 = 2,520 years.
3) In 1917 Balfour Declaration opened Palestine to Jews. 1917 was also Moslem year 1335 (see Dan 12:12). Dr Gratton-Guinness calculated correctly 31 years before fulfilment.

Learn Numbers 14:21: 'Truly as I live, all the earth shall be filled with the Glory of the Lord.'

JESUS IN THE PSALMS

I have mentioned a few prophecies of Jesus in the Psalms. They are so remarkable that they are worthy of a section on them alone.

'Christ' named

These prophecies are not so often studied, yet they are very significant indeed. Many of them were written by David about 1,000 years before Christ fulfilled them. Listen to Christ's own opinion about them! He said that 'David was inspired by the Holy Spirit' (Mt 22:43); that 'everything which had been written about him in the Psalms must be fulfilled' (Lk 24:44).

There are about ten psalms which prophesy about the Lord Jesus and they give over 30 details about the birth, life, the cross, resurrection, ascension and eternal priesthood of Jesus. That is quite a lot of detail isn't it from 1,000 years before they were fulfilled? The details are remarkable ones too.

The second psalm starts us off. Its fulfilment is quoted in the New Testament letter to the Hebrews. Did you know that the name of Christ appears first in this psalm? The word 'Christ' is the Greek word for 'anointed one'. That is why, in the New Testament, when it is quoted, it says, 'The Lord and his Christ'. In the Old Testament your translation probably says, 'The Lord and his anointed'.

In the Gospels you read in many places of people chatting and asking, 'Do you think this is the Christ?' That was the word in common parlance. When Jesus asked the Pharisees whose son they thought Christ would be, they knew perfectly that Jesus was referring to all the prophecies which called him, 'the anointed one'. Everybody in Jesus' day used the Greek translation of the Old Testament and that translation had the name 'Christ' where the Hebrew had 'the anointed one'.

CHECKPOINTS

JESUS IN THE PSALMS

1. **Ten Psalms** Give 30 details, 1,000 years before fulfilment.
   'David wrote of me – inspired by the Holy Spirit' (Mt 22:43).

2. **Called 'Christ'** which means anointed (Mt 26:63).
   'The LORD and his anointed' (Ps 2:2) or 'his Christ' (Ps 45:7).

3. **Rejected by earth's rulers** (Ps 2:2); rulers plot against Christ.

4. **Begotten from the dead. When?**
   'This day' – the Resurrection day (Ps 2:7).
   Rejected stone became head, on the Lord's day (Ps 118:17–26).
   Will return (Ps 118:26).
   'First-born from the dead' (Col 1:18).
   'This God fulfilled by raising Jesus from the dead, as it is written [in Ps 2], you are my Son, This day have I begotten you' (Ac 13:33).
   First in order of resurrection; 'first-born from the dead' (1 Cor 15:23).
   'First-born from the dead' (Rev 1:15).

5. **Pre-existence**
   The Son existed before this from eternity: 'I am' (Jn 8:58).

6. **Earthly reign**
   'The earth your possession . . . you will rule with a rod of iron' (Ps 2:7–9).
   'Rod of iron' to be experienced by opponents of Christ (Rev 19:15).
   'He will sit on his glorious throne' (Mt 25:31).
   Lord's Prayer 'Your kingdom come . . . on earth' (Mt 6:10).
   'Your throne is forever and ever' (Ps 45:6).

7. His gracious words prophesied in Psalm 45

'Grace poured into your lips' (Ps 45:2).

'Gracious words' (Lk 4:22); 'No one spoke like this man' (Jn 7:46).

'Fairer' Hebrew word used twice. 'Beautiful, beautiful'; lovely character.

'A sceptre of righteousness, is the sceptre of his kingdom' (v 6).

Myrrh (v 8) anoints for his death on the cross.

Cassia anoints bread for lovely taste. Bread of life satisfies Aloes gives fragrance to those near Christ.

8. Marriage of the Bride Psalm 45:9–17.

i.e. Those won to Christ (Rev 19:7–9).

THE MISSING WORDS

Do you enjoy supplying missing words in a competition? I do! Lots of people spend hours supplying the missing letters in a crossword puzzle.

Did you know that the Bible has a missing-words puzzle for you? It is in Psalm 40.

What do you do when working on a crossword? You look at the clues! Where should you look for the clues in the Bible? Well, in the New Testament, of course. In this case, you will find the clue where this verse is quoted in the New Testament. It is the letter to the Hebrews chapter 10 verse 5. 'Sacrifice and offering you did not desire.'

The next words should supply the missing ones in the Old Testament. What are they? 'A body you have prepared for me.'

How remarkable! Remarkable because that Psalm 40 was a prophecy made by David, 1,000 years before Jesus came to fulfil it!

But can we be sure that the words in the New Testament were not added after they were fulfilled? Do you know how we can know they were the genuine original words? It is because they were in the Greek translation of the Old Testament, and this Greek translation was made 288 years before Christ came, and that was the version all the people used in Christ's time. Yes, those words are there. 'A body you have prepared for me.' So what a great solution to the missing words. They could be a solution to words missing in someone's life! Could they be these? 'Lord Jesus, thank you that your body was prepared for suffering in my place. I accept forgiveness through your sacrifice.'

CHECKPOINTS

PROPHETIC PSALMS 22, 40, 110 AND 118

Psalm 40

Supply the missing words from Psalm 40:46:
(Jewish Hebrew copy of AD 900 had lost the words)
'Sacrifice you did not desire . . . .
burnt offering and sin offering you have not required.'

- Clue from New Testament Greek in Hebrews 10:5: Sacrifice you did not desire *soma de katertiso moi*
- Clue from Old Testament Greek LXX translated 280 BC Sacrifice you did not desire *soma de Katertiso moi*
- Clue from the Dead Sea Scrolls 100 BC agrees. So they supply the words which are missing from the Hebrew copy of AD 900.

The English translation is: *But a body you prepared for me.*

Significance of Psalm 40

David 1000 BC heard the second person of the Trinity prophesy that a body would be prepared for him (by virgin conception) to be sacrificed for our sins.
'And in the volume of the book it is prophesied of me.'

What volume was that?

Up to David's time it was the Pentateuch, Joshua, Judges, to 1 Kings. Scrolls were by Moses, Joshua and Samuel, all put in the sanctuary (Deut 31:24–26; Josh 24:26; 1 Sam 10:25). Moses wrote of atoning sacrifice and Samuel of Kingship.

Psalm 22

Describes in detail the suffering of Christ on the cross. Mark each detail. Can you find twenty-four?

Psalm 118

Three things prophesied: the joyful Resurrection, the Lord's day, and foundation stone for faith.

Psalm 110

Ascension to God's right hand until his return; and our present advocate. It is a private conversation in heaven which David overheard. The Father and the Son were discussing future plans.

33 THE FUTURE FORETOLD

WHAT GOD FORETOLD TO HOSEA

Most commentaries miss the main point of Hosea's tragedy. It is that, even as Hosea places his wife on probation for a long time, so God would place Israel on probation for over two millennial days in their dispersion.

God's broken home

Did you know that God had a broken home and a broken heart? This will help you if you have experienced this close at hand. Today, most families have had an experience of this in some way – either one of their sons or daughters has experienced it, or a relative, or sadly their own marriage has been threatened.

Yes, I said that God had a broken home. That is what he told Hosea the prophet.

> 'O the pain of it!' said God. 'I had a wife who left me her husband, and she became a prostitute, not once, not twice, but three times. And now I have still taken her back but this time I have put her on probation.'

> 'But Hosea, you must show compassion and forgiveness for your unfaithful wife; for I will show compassion for Israel, after she has learnt her lesson, after her period of probation. Her period of probation will be 2,500 years and I will bring back her sons. I will not be defeated! I will win them back in the end. Where once I said, "You are not my wife or my sons", there (back in Israel) I will say, "My wife" and she will say, "My husband".'

> 'He has torn us and he will heal us. He has smitten us and he

will bandage us up.' God said, 'This hurt me more than it hurt you,' and he says the same to individuals. He says the same to you. 'Afterwards the children of Israel will return and seek the LORD their God.'

So you have seen that if you have had the agony of a broken home or children with broken homes, God shares the agony. He will heal your backslidings, he says, he loves you freely.

There will be a happy ending to your story, even as we see God today working out a happy ending for Israel.

CHECKPOINTS

WHAT GOD FORETOLD TO HOSEA

1. **Significance missed** by most commentaries:
That just as Hosea put his unfaithful wife on probation, so God was going to put unfaithful Israel on probation for 2 millennial days (6:2) until purified by persecution, then they would return to Palestine.

2. **Hosea the first prophet**
775 BC to apply warnings of Leviticus 26 (Seven Times) dispersion. Northern 10 tribes, called Ephraim or Israel, were worse than Judah.

3. **Brief prophesied history in chapter one**
   • Ephraim will go into captivity before Judah (v 6).
   • Judah to be saved (v 7) from Assyria's invasion, by divine intervention not by arms (fulfilled 2 Kgs 19:6–8).
   • God would bring them back, even as Hosea would win back his wife. They would return to The Land where God had disowned them (v 10).
   • Both Ephraim and Judah would return to the Holy Land under 'One Head' (v 11) in the latter days (Ezek 37:15–23).

4. **Probation period chapter 3 onwards**
To be purified by persecution.
Remarkable fulfilment predicted in 3:4–5.
   • Israel has existed without king or country
   • without idolatry
   • without sacrifices (they ended in AD 70)
   • without priests (ended AD 70).
They are returning to Palestine in the Latter Days.
Their loving God will welcome back the prodigal Israel. 'I will heal their backslidings. I will love them freely' (14:4).

5. **Replacements during probation prepared for the gospel**
Synagogues replaced temple.
Rabbis replaced priests.
Christ's Atonement replaced animal sacrifices.

EZEKIEL'S FATAL HAIRCUT

Tied up in Ezekiel's hair was the world's history and Israel's destiny. Let your hair down by reading the clues which God gives to those of a teachable spirit.

The hair-raising illustration is in Ezekiel 5. God gave an outline of history which was still in the future for Ezekiel. The rest of the prophecy was worked out in chronological order throughout the rest of the book, and intertwined with it is the departure and return of God's glory to the Holy Land.

The first chapter opens with the vision of God's glory hovering over Jerusalem. Reluctantly his glory moves out stage by stage. Each stage gives Judah an opportunity to respond to God's pleading, but it always falls on deaf ears. Finally the glory departs from the Mount of Olives. It only returns there at the end of the age in chapter 43.

At what point have today's events reached in this order? We are at the end of chapter 37 with Israel back in the Holy Land with the two tribes and ten tribes united as one nation. The next events to be fulfilled are described in chapters 38 to 48.

It may be asked, 'Were these chapters of Ezekiel which were written so long ago, meant to refer to our times?' The answer is 'yes'. It is admitted that the invasion described in chapters 38 and 39 have never yet happened. This confirms the scripture which says it will be fulfilled 'after many days . . . in the latter years,' and it will be when Israel has returned and settled down in 'God's Land' after a long period of desolation (38:8, 12).

The nations in chapter 38 verses 2–6 have been identified in *Young's Concordance*, *Hasting's Dictionary* and by Professor H. Hawkes of Oxford who is an authority on East European ethnology. Those north of the Black Sea were of the Halstatt horse culture. Others were Iran, Iraq, Libya, Ethiopia, Somaliland, and Germany.

CHECKPOINTS

WHAT GOD FORETOLD TO EZEKIEL

A hair-raising prophecy
Chapter 5, a comprehensive prophecy from Ezekiel for 26 centuries. The prophet's hair, divided into three portions, represents Israel's future.

1. Two portions represent those burnt or slain in the invasion of 603 to 586 BC (v 2).
2. One third of Judah will survive but is scattered to the winds (v 12 and 22:15).
3. A little hair is rescued from that scattered, symbolising a remnant who would return to Jerusalem after 70 years exile 533 BC (v 3).
4. Even these the prophet then throws into the fire. The Romans will scatter them because they reject Christ (v 4). Fulfilled by Fall of Jerusalem AD 70.
5. All the scattered third will return to Israel at the end of the age. It began in 1917.

Note: Principle that a prophetic day equals one year is in chapter 4.

Fits into theme of God's glory, which structures the whole prophecy.

Opening vision of glory chapter 1. Stage by stage glory reluctantly departs as Judah refuses to repent of her cruel and horrible practices and idolatry.

1st: The glory lifts up from the ark (chapter 9).

2nd: From the sanctuary entrance to the East gate (10:18).

3rd: From the Mount of Olives the glory departs (11:23).

Meanwhile

Israel will have little sanctuaries (synagogues) through the world (11:16).

Israel is left as a valley of dry bones (37:1).

Israel is revived and return as united 12 tribes to Holy Land (37:15–23).

When settled they will be invaded (Armageddon?).

Israel will recognise the Lord and pagan nations are judged (39:21).

'They will see my glory' at the return of Christ.

4th: The glory returns via Olivet on the East (43:1) cf. Zech 14:4; Acts 1:11,12.

5th: Through the East gate 'The earth shone with his glory'

6th: Into the house of the Lord 'Lo! The glory of the Lord filled the house.' 'Son of man, this is the place of my throne' (43:5,6; Mt 25:31,32).

WHAT GOD TOLD DANIEL: THE GENTILE FUTURE

The formation of a States of Europe soon before Christ's return is also a sign given. It has been so clear in holy Scripture that believers have written about it for the last hundred years, e.g. the fourth empire of Daniel's image in chapter 2 is the iron Roman Empire.

This is divided into two as depicted by the two legs, the western and the eastern Empire; then the ten toes depict an amalgamation of those countries in the last days.

It is soon before the return of Christ, because God said, 'In the days of those kings, he will set up a kingdom which will never be destroyed.' How? It will be by the stone uncreated which will descend from heaven and smash the image on its toes. The toes represent the last European power to exist before Christ's descent from heaven.

This amalgam of European powers will be that of separate sovereign states, because it says, 'In the days of those kings'. Note the plural. That is why when the picture is repeated in Revelation 13, the one crown is taken from the one emperor and placed as separate crowns upon each of the ten heads of the beast. It is interesting that even European nations, most of which have no king as such, still refer to themselves as sovereign states.

First coming or second coming?

How do we know that this stone which smashed the image on its feet means the second coming and not the first? It is because at his second coming, Christ will descend visibly from heaven. That is what the stone did. He did not do that at his first coming. He came then as a baby – as God incarnate.

Another sign that this refers to the second coming is that it is to happen later in history, after the height of Rome's power. The Roman Empire, Daniel said, will have become divided and then split into many European countries and finally an amalgamation of several countries into a States of Europe. It is 'in the days of those powers', that the uncreated stone descends from heaven and smashes the image of man's governmental systems and sets up a kingdom of godliness, righteousness and happiness.

The time of the Gentiles

Did you know that Jesus called the Emperor's dream statue in the book of Daniel, 'the time of the Gentiles'? It is those 25 centuries since the Babylonian Empire down to our day which the Lord Jesus Christ calls the time of the Gentiles (see Lk 21:24).

Why is it called, 'The time of the Gentiles'? It is because during that time, Gentiles have ruled in Jerusalem. Its duration is the same period as the dispersion of Israel. For the same 25 centuries, the Israelites have been scattered among countries other than their own, as prophesied.

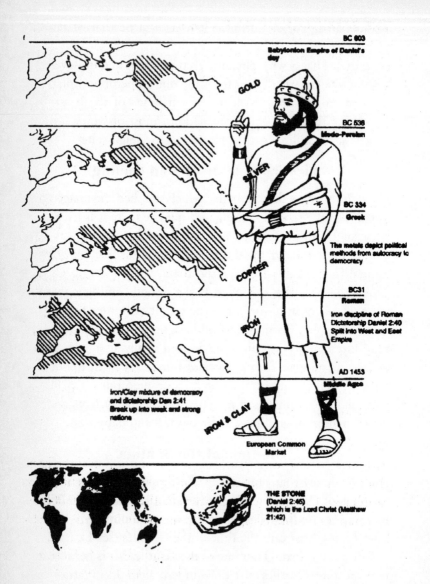

Fig. 24. Daniel's image prophesying history from 603 BC to the present day in which the toes represent European sovereignties. The stone strikes the toes 'in the days of these sovereignties' at Christ's return to rule the world.

THE LANGUAGE OF BABYLON

At one time, the critics said that Daniel could not have written chapters 2:4 to end of chapter 8 because the Aramaic speech was not known until later. But there again they were wrong. Archaeology has shown that Aramaic was spoken before Daniel's time. In any case, chapter 1 of Daniel tells you that Daniel and his friends were to be taught Aramaic as part of their re-education. It was the language of Babylon.

Another passage in the Bible also shows that Aramaic was spoken long before Daniel – 200 years in fact. This is in 2 Kings 18:26. It was when good King Hezekiah was besieged in Jerusalem by the triumphant Assyrian armies. The enemy general started shouting threats to the defenders on the walls of Jerusalem in their Hebrew language. He told them that Jehovah could not defend them. He was trying to create a mutiny. The king's messenger said, 'Don't speak in Hebrew but speak in Aramaic (that was the Syrian language) for we understand it.' Now if the Bible says that Aramaic was spoken as early as that, I believe the Bible, but archaeology also confirms it. Arthur Gibson of Manchester University shows from the Dere Ala tablets that Aramaic was known well before Daniel's time.

Sovereign teaching

The book of Revelation proclaims this teaching amidst the backcloth of thunder and lightning, roaring seas and scorching sun, earthquakes and the sound of trumpets. The rise and fall of kings and empires is summed up by this comment in Revelation 17:17.

> God has put it into their hearts to fulfil his purpose, to be of one mind in giving their kingdom to the beast, until the words of God are fulfilled.

Consequently, whether the emperor was good or bad, Peter said in 1 Peter 2:13,14, 'Submit yourselves to every ordinance of man for the Lord's sake, whether to the king as supreme, or to governors . . . for this is the will of God, that by doing good you may silence the ignorant misrepresentations of foolish men.'

Paul likewise said in Romans 13:1–2, 'Be subject unto the authorities . . . for they are ordained by God.'

Concerning the prophesied future, he wrote, 'He who now restrains, will do so until he is removed, and then the lawless one will be revealed whom the Lord will consume away with the breath of his mouth [his inspired word] and finally destroy with the brightness of his coming.'

CHECKPOINTS

WHAT GOD FORETOLD TO DANIEL

The Gentile future and prophesied history of the Four Empires from 603 BC to 20th century

Note: the Aramaic language was in use well before Daniel's time

Images of the Empires (Dan 2)	*Animal Symbols of Empires (Dan.7)*
Head of Gold = Babylon 603–538 BC	Deflated Lion = Nebuchadnezzar humbled by madness
Arms and Chest of Silver = Medo-Persia 538–334 BC	Lop-sided Bear = Persia stronger than Media. 3 ribs: Egypt, Babylon, Lydia defeated
Waist of Bronze = Greece 334–31 BC	Leopard with 4 wings = Alexander who dies and 4 generals divide Empire
Legs of Iron = Rome 31 BC to 20th century AD. Divides into E and W like the legs then into 10 (toes) at the end (European single market with 10 ethnic groupings?).	The Horror Beast with iron teeth. Europe breaks up into 10 'kingdoms'. Little horn propaganda uproots 3 kingdoms. After 3½ times (1,260 years) Bible is read again and gradually corrects errors (7:25,26).

Uncreated stone descends from Heaven in days of ten toes and smashes the Image.	Son of Man descends with the clouds

God's sovereignty is the prime teaching in Daniel. Man proposes but God disposes, or 'human randomness mutates into Divine teleology (purpose)'.

Each episode reaches this conclusion:
- Daniel's image 2:21: 'God removes kings and sets up kings'.
- Monarch's madness 4:32: 'The Most High overrules in the kingdoms of men'.
- Writing on the wall 5:21: 'The Most High overrules in the kingdoms of men'.
- Lion's den 6:26,27: 'God's Kingdom cannot be destroyed'.
- Horror Beast 7:21–27: Wears out saints only until 'Judgement sits'.
- Waiting for Messiah 9:24: 'Seventy weeks of years are *determined*'.

NT applies this sovereign teaching
'God has put it into their hearts to fulfil his will . . . until' (Rev 17); 'Submit yourselves . . . unto governors as sent by him (1 Pet 2:13,14); 'Be subject unto the authorities . . . they are ordained by God, (Rom 13:1,2).

WHAT GOD FORETOLD TO DANIEL: IN HEBREW CONFI DENTIALITY

Will the Jews rebuild the temple?

Chapters 8 to 12 are an answer to the question, 'When will the sanctuary be cleansed?' In answering this, it involves the Jewish future and is therefore confidential. This is why Daniel was inspired to write these chapters in the old Hebrew which was no longer in general use, but understood by Jews.

The future fortunes of the Jews and the Sanctuary where the temple stood were in an area which was going to be invaded by the Greek king, Alexander the Great, 200 years after God told Daniel about it. That is why the scene is set in the area which was going to be covered by the Greek Empire. This empire was symbolised by the goat which is appropriate because the sea between Greece and Turkey is called the Goat Sea, or Aegean in the Greek. After AD 638, the area of the former Greek Empire was occupied by Muslim powers who extended their conquests to Yugoslavia and the Balkans in AD 1453. So these prophecies extend down to our time.

HISTORIC PURPOSES

In the prophecies God gave to Daniel, we have seen the purpose behind each empire down the last 2,500 years. You see, God didn't foretell the future just to satisfy curiosity. It was to show his purpose behind history.

The Persian Empire restored a remnant of godly people back to Palestine after 70 years, as foretold by Jeremiah. The temple was rebuilt and so were the city walls. That remnant established Jewry which prepared for Christ's first coming.

The Greek Empire which followed – what was God's purpose for them? What language was your New Testament written in? It was Greek. All translations of the New Testament are translations from the Greek, which had become the international language of the day.

Alexander the Great spread his conquests East and West.

Even in Egypt the language became Greek. That is why the Old Testament became translated into Greek 280 years before Christ. By the time of Christ, the Greek version of the Old Testament was widely used even by the Jews. It was from this translation that all the Christians quoted when they wrote the New Testament.

The surprising thing is that even when the Greek Empire gave way to the Roman Empire, the international language still continued to be Greek, which is why Paul and others had this international language to use when they travelled through Europe.

So what about the Roman Empire? How did God use that iron empire? Rome's iron might removed all national barriers. Passports were not needed to pass from country to country. Rome's roads, too, took the traveller from one end of Europe to another. Paul was able to travel freely to bring the good news of salvation and as did the other Christians.

Remember that the prophecies of Daniel said that the Roman Empire would later divide up into East and West and then the West into about ten countries. This it has done, so what purpose did God have in that? Was it not so that these European countries could send explorers throughout the world? Unintentionally that opened up the world for Christians to take the good news. When the countries fail to help the gospel, God withdraws his blessing. If we look at history through Bible eyes, we shall understand.

CHECKPOINTS

GOD'S COMPUTER ANGEL – PALMONI

1. Palmoni means 'the wonderful numberer of prophetic secrets' – the name of a special angel whose job is to give the length of time in which certain prophecies will be fulfilled, to answer those who ask 'how long?' (Dan 8:13).
2. Translators merely say 'an angel or saint'.
3. When Daniel is distressed in 6 BC that the temple sanctuary is destroyed, Palmoni is sent to tell him restoration will start after 2,300 evenings and mornings from the time Alexander the Great invades Jerusalem.
4. This was fulfilled by the Six-Day War in 1967, when general Dyan captured the temple site. Alexander invaded in 333 BC and Dyan reached the Wailing Wall 2,300 years later. (This was anticipated by Adam Clarke as long ago as AD 1820.)

FALSE CHRISTS AND FALSE PROPHETS

Many are appalled at the rise of false christs and false prophets; but Jesus said this would happen soon before his return.

> 'Many will come in my name saying I am Christ, and will deceive many . . . and many false prophets will rise and will deceive many.' (Matthew 24:5,11).

Jesus says that deception would be their chief objective (see v 25). He warns that some would be so like the real thing that if it were possible it would even deceive 'the true elect'.

Jesus also knew that during history Christianity would become divided, and he warned his disciples about it. Yet he trusted his Good News of salvation to the care of failing folk nevertheless. He knew also that later on in history there would arrive imitations of the real thing which would promote Christianity as a religion by force of the sword instead of his method of kindness, love and forgiveness; and even martyrdom with torture and death. This is why the saying arose, 'the blood of the martyrs is the seed of the church'. The situation would be even more confusing when political power was given to religion.

Daniel and Revelation reveal that this would last for 1,260 years in one case and 1,335 periods in the other. Details about this are in my book, *Evidence for Truth: Prophecy.* One persecuting power would be in the former Western Roman Empire and the other in the former Eastern Roman Empire.

The political Christian power in the West was instituted in AD 610 by Emperor Phocas and taken away in 1870. So, according to Dr Gratton Guinness and others, we are now in the period described in Daniel 8:23–25 and 2 Thessalonians 2:3–8, when their errors would be 'first gradually consumed by the Word of Christ's mouth and then suddenly by the brightness of his return'.

What should be the response of Bible-believing Christians now that we are living in that correction period? Should it not be one of fellowship and sharing the truth of the Bible with others? A significant step was taken by the Roman Catholics before the Second World War. They gave permission to their own followers to read translations of the Bible in their own tongue. Years before, they had even burnt believers io death with their Bibles round their necks. Now recently in one South American country they have actually authorised the use of a translation for which originally they burnt to death the translator. With the gentleness of a modern pope who is very different from the mediaeval types, Christ's way of love and forgiveness is the only method authorised by Jesus and being practised by *true* Christians.

So we should encourage fellowship with Roman Catholics. I have enjoyed fellowship with those who are testing their beliefs by the Bible. Many have had their eyes opened to trust in the full salvation won by Christ alone through his completed redemption made once for all time on the Cross.

The prophecies say that the area of the False Prophet would also be affected. The Bible will bring those in the East gradually to forsake their errors. It is significant that countries from Turkey eastwards can listen to Christian programmes on radio and television in spite of prohibitions.

Many Chrisitans have debated whether these prophecies should be applied to history or to the future, but both applications apply in any case to the gradual reduction of error near the end of the age.

'A time' is the name given to a measurement used in ancient history. Its value is 360 and this is why we have 360 degrees in a circle. So the period referred to in Daniel 7:25 adds up as follows: One time = 360, 2 times = 720 and a half time = 180, **TOTAL = 1,260**. It is also referred to in Daniel 12:7 and Revelation 12:14 & 11:3. Leviticus 26:28 refers to twice that length prophesying the 7 times (2,520 years) of Israel's absence from Palestine until their return in the twentieth century.

THE FALSE CHRIST AND THE FALSE PROPHET

Chapters 7 and 8 of Daniel as applied in the book of Revelation and by Paul in 2 Thessalonians 2 reveal that true Christians would be severely devastated by two false religious systems called the False Christ and the False Prophet. Chapter 7 has been seen to be about the False Christ who operates in the former *Western* Roman Empire. The Little Horn depicts the False Christ which arose as a power in Western Europe after the demise of the ten powers (the ten horns) replacing the Western Empire. Three identifications are given.

1. The power will prevail and wear out the saints.
2. He shall change times and seasons; this was arranged by the pope in the eighteenth century, when a calendar correction of a few days was introduced. Britain refused to make the change and stuck to the old calendar for many years.
3. Heavenly judgement will take away his political power.

The papal political power ceased in 1870 which was 1,260 years after it was given by the last emperor of Rome in AD 610.

It is thought therefore that this political power will return to the more scriptural spirituality which it had before its political status was granted. This fulfils the two stages: first gradual consumption of error and second by the return of Christ when all error will be destroyed (Daniel 7:26; 2 Thessalonians 2:8). Others take this as referring to the last seven years of the end of the age.

Chapter 8 of Daniel refers to the False Prophet who was to arise in the former *Eastern* Roman Empire because the sanctuary of Jerusalem is in the Eastern Roman province. Alexander the Great is referred to because he first conquered that area by force of arms. The language of Daniel 8:23–24 is mysterious because that is the area which would later be subject to a mysterious philosophy rather than military arms. Daniel 8:23–26 reads as follows:

> And in the latter time of their kingdom, when the transgressors are come to the full, a king of fierce countenance, and understanding dark sentences, shall stand up. And his power shall be mighty, but not by his own power: and he shall destroy wonderfully (mystically), and shall prosper and practise and shall destroy the mighty and the holy people. And through his policy also he shall cause craft to prosper in his hand; and he shall magnify himself in his heart, and by peace shall destroy many: he shall also stand up against the Prince of Princes (Jesus Christ); but he shall be broken without hand. And the vision of the evening and the morning which was told is true: wherefore shut thou up the vision; for it shall be for many days.

Notice the reference to the 2,300 'evenings and mornings' given by Palmoni mentioned above. Jesus referred to this appearance of the False Prophet as one who will demand pilgrimages into the desert (see Matthew 24:26).

So the False Prophet would become the dominant mystical power in the Eastern Empire and the False Christ would dominate the old Western section of the Roman Empire from Rome. Sir Isaac Newton, applying Daniel, said that the political power of both deceptions would last for 1,260 years after which there will be a slow disappearance of the two deceptions through the 'word of Christ's mouth', i.e. the Bible and finally, suddenly by the second coming of Christ.

CHECKPOINTS

CONFIDENTIAL HEBREW LANGUAGE ABOUT JEWS' FUTURE

Temple sanctuary cleansing, chapters 8 to 12 of Daniel.
God's Computer Angel named Palmoni 'wonderful calculator'.
The Sanctuary was in the former Greek Empire (Dan 8:21,22).

Palmoni says 2,300 years before cleansing begins.

333 BC to 1967 AD = 2,300 years. Wailing Wall made a synagogue. Sanctuary Cycle is an amazing cycle (M. de Cheseaux's astronomical discovery). It is a unit of astronomical time in which the sun and the moon return to their juxtaposition.

Three Abominations:
1. Antiochus Epiphanes 167 BC sacrilege in temple (Dan 8:23).
2. Fall of Jerusalem. Roman and Zealot sacrilege of temple. Jesus and Daniel spoke of another after no.1 (Mt 24:15).
3. Mosque 'standing where it ought not' AD 638 (Dan 11:31). But some refer it to the tribulation.

Messiah dated 70 weeks of days, i.e. 490 years (Dan 9:25,26) **fulfilled:**

457 BC Cyrus commands building of temple (Dan 9:25 and Ezra 1:2) + 490 **solar** years = AD 33 the Cross.
444 BC Artaxerxes commands building of the walls + 490 **lunar** years = AD 33 (Neh 2:1,5).
Christ was crucified in the middle of the last week of years, i.e. after $3^1/2$ years ministry; that reduces AD 33 to AD 30.

Signs of Christ's second coming in Daniel chapter 12
1. When resurrection of believers is near (12:2).
2. Terrible time of trouble (12:1).
3. Increased travel, invention and science for many (12:4).
4. It will be the end of 7 times – $3^1/2$ x 2 – (12:7) in 20th century.

5. Great increase in wickedness (12:10) but bright witnessing.
6. From Muslim date to blessing Israel 1335 = 1917. Home for Jews (12:11,12).
7. The wise will understand these figures in the last days (12:9,10).

DANIEL'S SEVENTY WEEKS OF YEARS

Chapter 9 verses 24–27

1. Daniel was anxious to know when the Messiah would come and restore God's honour in the sanctuary at Jerusalem. God's reply to him through the angel was that it would be 490 years after a certain starting date until the Messiah appeared on earth. Many people get confused on how the dates actually work out because they do not realise that there are several starting dates that are fulfilled in several events. Look first at the terminal events which Daniel 9:24–27 forecasts. They were:

i. Christ's baptism at which the Holy Spirit anointed him in AD 27;
ii. The atoning death of Jesus on the cross in AD 33;
iii. The destruction of Jerusalem and the temple in AD 70;
iv. The end of all animal sacrifices in Jewish ritual in AD 70;
v. According to *some* interpretations, the erection of the Mosque of Omar on the old temple site in AD 638.

From these starting dates given to Daniel there are four or five fulfilment events.

2. **Fulfilment events**
In fulfilment, I think it best if I take those verses piece by piece, so turn to your Bible, Daniel 9:24–27.

Verse 24:   Daniel's 70 weeks of years, i.e. 70 x 7 = 490 years.
Verse 24a: The cross is prophesied, 'End of sins and reconciliation for sinners'.

Verse 24b: 'To anoint the most holy', i.e. to baptise sinless Jesus. At baptism Jesus was anointed by the Holy Spirit.

Verse 25a: The command to rebuild the walls of Jerusalem in 457 BC given by emperor Artaxerxes to the Messiah (Christ) will be 7 weeks, i.e. 49 years (it took 49 years to rebuild the city because of opposition). 'Rebuilding will be in troublous times.'

Verse 25b: So the next starting date would be 62 weeks later in 408 BC. That, plus AD 27 comes to the baptism (anointing Christ means Anointed One).

Verse 26a: 'Messiah will be crucified for *others*.'

Verse 26b: The 'Prince' or 'Emperor' who came to destroy the city was Titus. He burnt the city to the ground. But it was the prince's soldiers who burnt the temple against Titus' orders. This was God's overruling so that no more sacrifices would be offered. This was to indicate that the Christ had made all other sacrifices unnecessary. His atonement was sufficient for everyone who accepted his salvation. It was in the middle of 7 years, which was the length of Christ's ministry.

Verse 26c: Until the return of Christ ('until the end of the age') a series of desolations will continue.

Verse 27a: A further interpretation is possible for v 27 that the temple site will be further desecrated by an abomination.

Verse 27b: 'A canopy of blasphemy will be erected over the site.' The Mosque of Omar was built over Abraham's rock upon which the temple rested. Around the dome there is an inscription, saying 'God has **no** son', quoted from the Koran. The Hebrew is canopy meaning high ormnamental hard cover over an important site, like the Dome of the Rock. St John's first letter chapter 4 verses 1–3 says, 'He who denies the Son is the antichrist.'

Verse 27c: At the end of the age the antichrist will make a 7-year pact with the Jews and then break it after three and a half years (in the middle of the week of years).

3. There is also another time schedule that has been worked out in lunar years, i.e. the number of times the moon has waxed and waned. Four hundred and ninety lunar years from the decree also takes us to the ministry of Christ.

4. Apparently, Sir Isaac Newton, the great scientist and astronomer, found other interesting factors. For example, he found that there were 6,000 lunations from 457 BC to AD 29 and that that reflected fulfilment of the meaning of the feasts of the year in Exodus chapter 24 verses 14–17. This outlines the three main Church festivals and Israelite feasts, namely, the Passover, the Feast of Harvest and the Ingathering at the end of the year. There were, indeed, 600 lunations between the Feast of Jubilee to the Day of Atonement. One lunation was the time between the two new moons. As you know, these three main feasts, which God gave, were prophecies of the death, resurrection and ascension of the Lord Jesus Christ. Newton saw a fulfilment in the interval between 457 BC, which was the starting point of calculation, and the Ascension of Jesus, which was 6,000 lunations.

So you see that 600 lunations in the Jewish and Church year of services, was prophetic of 6,000 lunations from 457 BC to the return of Jesus to heaven at the Ascension.

An enlargement of the Hebrew of Daniel 9:26–27

After the decree by Emperor Artaxerxes in 457 BC to rebuild the walls of Jerusalem, the city will take 49 years to rebuild owing to stops and starts in troublous times caused by opposing peoples. Then, after the remaining 434 years, the anointed Christ will be killed but not for himself (on the cross for us sinners).

Then the emperor of an empire still to come will destroy the city of Jerusalem, and his soldiers, contrary to orders, will destroy the temple (AD 70).

From that time on a flood of war and destruction are decreed to the end of the age.

During that time a canopy of blasphemy will cover the holy

site and continue to do so to the end of the age, but in God's foreordained time, his judgement will be poured out upon these desolaters. The authority will make a treaty with the Jews to allow them to make sacrifices and offerings for seven years but after three and a half years he will break his agreement and cause the sacrifices to cease. (This will probably cause Armageddon to begin.)

WHAT GOD FORETOLD TO ZECHARIAH

Introduction to Zechariah – an astonishing state ment

I want to draw out your imagination of the events which led up to the next to last book of the Old Testament. It is the book of the prophet Zechariah, a dramatic book, written from 520 to 517 BC. **It actually pictures Jehovah being crucified on the cross.** The Hebrew says, 'It is me, Jehovah, whom they pierced', and 'The whole Israelite nation will be converted when they see it is me whom they crucified when I return to the Mount of Olives at the end of the age' (Zech 12:10; 14:3,4).

Earth-shaking events

I have already described God's geological knowledge in *Evidence for Truth* Volume 2. The earth-shaking events which are to happen at Christ's return are described to Ezekiel in such a way as to show that God knew all about the geology of this globe. It will involve the Great Rift Valley and the movement of continents. It reveals that the increase in earthquakes is the continents preparing to split at the moment Christ's feet touch the Mount of Olives at his descent. The dramatic results are described in Ezekiel 47 and in Zechariah 14.

Zechariah 14:4 says, 'On that day his feet will stand on the Mount of Olives which lies before Jerusalem on the East.'

Whose feet are these? Verse 3 tells you they are Jehovah's (which is translated 'The Lord'). In the New Testament you are told that they will be the feet of the Lord Jesus Christ. Clearly this implies that Jesus is Jehovah.

Now turn to Acts 1:11 and you read that two angels appeared to the disciples as the Lord Jesus ascended into heaven. They said, 'Men of Galilee, why do you stand looking into heaven? This same Jesus, who is taken up from you into heaven, will come in the same manner that you have seen him go into heaven.'

It is then that two great geological events will happen of cataclysmic proportions.

1. A great rift valley will open up past Jerusalem and link up the Mediterranean Sea with the Red Sea and the Indian Ocean.
2. Fresh water will be released from an artesian basin which is known to be under Jerusalem.

Now note that these events are associated with the Lord becoming king over all the earth (v 9). Why? Because it will make Jerusalem the maritime centre of the world. In fact Zechariah, like the other prophets, ends with Christ reigning in a millennium of peace for all creation.

CHECKPOINTS

WHAT GOD FORETOLD TO ZECHARIAH

List of prophecies about Jesus' first coming:
Palm Sunday: Jesus will ride on a donkey to the temple now being built (9:9).
He will be betrayed for 30 pieces of silver (11:12,13).
Jesus as God, the Good Shepherd (13:7).
He will be Jehovah whom they crucify (12:10).
He will be the chief stone of salvation bringing grace (4:7).
He is the Branch of David's fallen tree (3:8; 6:12).
He is Priest–King descended through Zerubbabel (6:13; 4:6–10; Mt 1:12).

Events of the last days described in the last four chapters:
1. Revival in the latter rain (10:1).
2. Return of Israel from all the world (10:10).
3. Lebanon's agony (11:1,2).
4. Problems of Jerusalem bring failure to politicians (12:3).
5. Army from all nations will attack Jerusalem (12:3).
6. Christ will suddenly descend to Mount Olivet (12:10; 14:4)
7. Israelis will recognise Christ's wounds (TV close-up?) (12:10).
8. Israel's sorrow, repentance and cleansing (12:10–14).
9. Christ will descend when city is half taken (14:1–4).
10. Olivet will split in two and Rift Valley will join up Mediterranean with Red Sea (14:4–8).
11. Christ will judge the world and reign over it (14:9).
12. Every nation will send up representatives to worship Jesus Christ at Harvest Festival time (14:16–19).
13. All advertisements, newspapers and TV will be cleansed and only propagate pure and wholesome things.

THE YEARLY SEASONS ARE PROPHESIED HISTORY

People ask 'Why does Easter come late sometimes?' Answer: Because the seasons Easter, Whitsun and Harvest are timed by the moon. They were given by God to Moses 1,400 years before Jesus fulfilled them.

They arose from the three seasons for the Israelite feasts. These were fulfilled in the life of Jesus by his death, resurrection and ascension which took place on those Jewish feasts and which are celebrated by the Church festivals on Good Friday, Easter and Pentecost (and Harvest). These were all measured by the moon.

The Jewish feasts given by God in the Bible in Exodus 23:14–17 and Leviticus 23:1–44 were:

- The Passover (which became Good Friday) March or April.
- The First Fruit Harvest (which became the Resurrection).
- The Day of Atonement and Ingathering, Final Harvest (Harvest Festivals/Easter Day) Sept–Oct.

The Israelite seasons became fulfilled exactly the same time as their celebrations beginning at the Passover and completing at the Ingathering harvest.

According to the famous scientist Sir Isaac Newton, the period from Passover to the final harvest, the moon waxed and waned 600 times (called lunations). That was prophetic because from Daniel's starting date of 457 BC to Christ's Ascension in AD 33 that was 6,000 lunations (Dan 9:24).

The times of the unfolding of these events are given in Scripture but not the date of Christ's return. Jesus made it quite plain that no one should pretend to know the date (Mk 13:32, Ac 1:7).

Why then does God give us time periods but not dates? It is to assure his people that he is working to a plan and towards a certain future. In the first section of Scripture Moses says,

> The secret things belong unto the LORD our God: but those things which are revealed belong unto us and to our children for ever, that we may do all the words of this law.
>
> Deut 29:29 (AV)

In the ensuing books of the Bible, God progressively reveals more and more of his remarkable plan. He reveals that he knows Israel will break their pledge with God. He reveals that Israel will be scattered among the nations for over two and a half thousand years, the seven times. He reveals that he will bring them back to the Holy Land. That remarkable event we saw started in 1917 (1335 Muslim date as in Daniel 12:12). The final season of harvest is approaching when he will reap his harvest and establish his kingdom on earth (Mt 25:31, 32).

A moon month is only 28 days long, and so a moon year is also shorter. That is why a Muslim date of 1335 is given in Daniel 12:12 for the blessing of Israel being granted residence in the Holy Land which was fulfilled in the Muslim moon date for what was 1335 – 1917. Muslims date from Mohammed's flight and Christians date from Christ's birth.

34 THE PRINCE OF PROPHETS

You will of course immediately recognise that the Prince of Prophets is the Lord Jesus. His major prophecy, given on the Mount of Olives, is the most remarkable outline of history ever predicted – and was to happen between his ascension and his return.

Many events he prophesied are now facts of history and others are unfolding before us, but some people get confused because they say there are all kinds of opinion about application. Others just weigh one opinion against another. This is not the way to get the truth from God's Word. Behind differing opinions, we should look for the motives and assumptions behind them. For example, some don't believe that the Lord Jesus will personally appear in the heavens. Others are more wedded to the passing fashions of theological thought.

So, to be subject to the insight of the Holy Spirit and carefully comparing scripture with scripture, we have to let self be crucified. St Paul says in 2 Corinthians 10:5, 'Cast down all theories and every pride that exalts itself . . . and bring into captivity every thought to obey Christ.'

So you see, it is not just a matter of weighing up man's opinions but noting carefully the terms of reference in the Scriptures themselves and subjecting even our own pet theories to Christ.

What are the terms of reference in what Jesus, the Prince of Prophets, said about the future? Turn with me to Matthew. This remarkable prophecy by the Lord himself is also reported in Mark 13 and Luke 21 but we will look now at Matthew 24:3. Here we find that the Lord Jesus answers three questions put to him by the disciples.

1. When will Jerusalem and the temple be destroyed?

2.   What will be the signs of your second coming?

3.   What will be the signs of the end of the age?

As a matter of fact, if we see that the Saviour was replying to those three questions, what he said outlines the history of the 2,000 years from his time to ours.

CHECKPOINTS

THE LORD JESUS CHRIST

Jesus answered 3 questions: 1. Jerusalem; 2. The Age; 3. The Second coming

Jesus Foretells 20 centuries of history in Matthew 24 and 25; Mark 13; Luke 21.

1. **When would Jerusalem fall?** (it was in AD 70)

    First the disciples would have to witness.

    Then there would be two stages in the Fall:

    'Wars of Jews' began, AD 67. Cestius surrounds the city.

    Christians must flee whole country because $3^1/_2$ years war would commence; this is recorded by Luke alone. AD 70, Titus would reach Jerusalem at Passover. Christians must flee over roof tops, last minute (Mt and Mk). Jews Tribulation follows and Jerusalem trodden down until AD 1967 (Lk 21:24)

2. **The Age** would not end until 'times of the Gentiles' ended (Lk 21:24). Two main apostacies would last 1,260 and 1,335 years: one in West 'inner rooms', one in East 'Prophet of Desert' (Mt 24:26).

    The Jewish Tribulation would last from the fall of Jerusalem until the second coming (Lk 21:22–24, Mt 24:21,29).

3. **Signs of second coming**

Space signs (Mt 24:29; Mk 13:24; Lk 21:25).

Increase in earthquakes, famine and epidemics.

World wars involving whole populations.

Organisation of nations to solve problems (Lk 21:25).

Uranium nuclear fission (heavens – Greek *uranos*) (Mk 13:25).

Phobias and stress a threat.

Fig tree (Israel) reviving and returning to 'God's Land'. Sign of Son of Man coming in the clouds (Mt 24:30; 25).

a. Wedding of Bride – i.e. The saved (resurrection; Mt 25:1–13).

b. Rewards and places in coming Kingdom (Mt 25:14–30).

c. Christ's throne on earth to judge nations. Kingdom on earth follows (Lk 21:31).

35 THE RISEN JESUS FORETELLS THE FUTURE

THE TRIUMPHAL ARCH OF REVELATION

At the entrance to Thessalonica in northern Greece, there is an ancient Arch of Triumph. It shows a series of pictures of the Emperor Galerius in AD 310. It was actually his last triumph because he was a cruel persecutor of Christians. Ironically, his huge tomb nearby became a meeting place for Christians and for a thousand years they met to praise and worship the triumphant Christ.

The last book in the Bible is like an arch of triumph – the triumph and victory of the Lord Jesus Christ. Likewise, there is a panel of pictures. Each panel ends in a victory for Jesus. That is why the book is called 'The Revelation' – the Revelation of Jesus Christ. That is what the opening words call this remarkable book: 'The Revelation of Jesus Christ which God gave unto him to show to his servant.'

As I studied the panels on that earthly triumphal arch, I saw there were some symbols which I didn't understand; but other pictures were quite clear in their meaning. For example, some soldiers were mounted on horses just as it is in the Revelation panel and at the end of each panel the emperor was in his victory chariot. It is the same in the book of Revelation. The Lord Jesus is on his triumphant throne or in his victory procession at the end of each panel. Then comes the final conquest and his eternal reign.

CHECKPOINTS

TRIUMPHAL ARCH OF REVELATION
Prophesies world history from 1st century to modern times

Analysis: Christ's triumphal arch has:
    Four panels. Each panel has seven pictures and ends with Christ's triumph.
    Between each panel there are given symbols to explain the meanings of the panels (e.g. Rev 17:1).

1st panel of seven lampstands i.e. Christian witness.
    Matthew 5:15; Zechariah 4; Revelation 1:20.
    1st to 20th century.
    Christ witnessing amidst seven church eras .
    Vision of heaven's control room chapters 4 and 5.

2nd panel, seven seals: Christ's triumph over Rome, chapters 6 and 7 AD 62–323.
    Symbol of the martyrs, Hebrew and Gentile 7:1–17.
    Short space of peace before apostacies persecute 8:1.

3rd panel, seven trumpets: persecution by the two apostacies, the False Christ and the False Prophet, chapters 8 to 10.
    Euphratean power floods out from East, 9:14 sixth trumpet.
    Causes the Reformation in the West, chapter 10.
    Four symbols to interpret the panel, chapters 11 to 14.

4th panel, seven cauldrons of wrath defeat the apostacies.
    Each cauldron is a reply to each trumpet in panel three.
    Euphratean power dries up. Chapter 16:12 sixth cauldron.
    Visions to explain the cauldrons 'One of the angels of the cauldrons came and said, "Come, I will show you . . ." ' (17:1).

Note The above is the **Historic** application of panels 1 to 4. The **Futuristic** fulfilment would be during the Tribulation. Prophecy is usually fulfilled both ways. i.e. symbolically and then literally (Mt 17:10–13).

SEVEN SISTERS

As I look along the beautiful cliffs towards Eastbourne on the south coast of England, I see the chalk cliffs which are called the Seven Sisters. The cliffs shine white in the sun and the glistening sea laps at their bases. The sea eats away this base so that the chalk rock falls straight down. This leaves the white chalk cliffs always vertical and at the top the fresh grass grows a green carpet right to the edge. This gives the top a wavy green line emphasising the seven white humps. These are the Seven Sisters divided by six dips. The last dip before the seventh hump is wider than the others. Indeed, it is called a gap – Birling Gap. When I get to it, I look through it and . . . the cliffs turn a corner. They start a new series of white cliffs.

Now, in the book of Revelation, the seven seals and the trumpets are like that. In both cases, there is a gap between the sixth and the seventh. Into that gap is put a symbol or vision. This is to give an insight into the next series of sevens to follow. It is as if to say: 'You expected the end to come didn't you, but no, there is another seven to come, before the end.'

This is to keep the Church expectant all down the ages. The Church which no longer expects her Lord to return is a Church which has fallen asleep. So said the Lord in his parable of the ten virgins.

What is that common feature in the seven trumpets? It is a time measurement. The prophecies of the seven trumpets concern a period of 1,260 days. Remember that Ezekiel was told that each day represented one year. So the seven trumpets concern a period of 1,260 years long.

The Kingdom has not been won yet. That won't happen until the rapture of the saved – that is, until the resurrection of those born again. 'Wait until we have sealed the complete number.'

Now, Ephesians 1:13 tells you what this sealing is. The believer is sealed by the Holy Spirit when he believes the gospel and is saved. Then chapter 4 verse 30 tells you that that sealing guarantees that the bodies of the saved will be changed and resurrected at the coming of Christ.

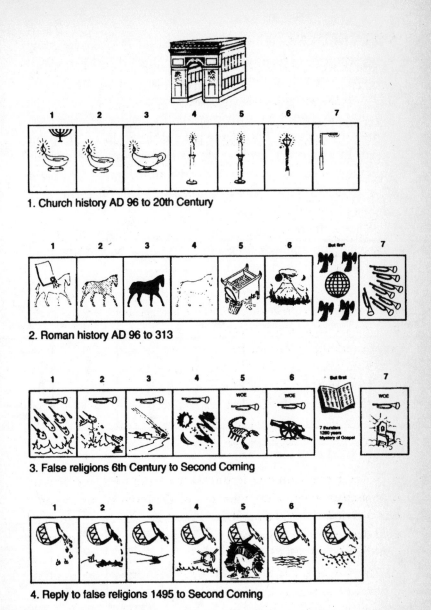

Fig. 25. Drawings of the four 'panels' of Revelation's 'Arch of Triumph' as suggested by the author, depicting seven lamps (the Church), seven seals (Roman Empire), seven trumpets (world powers) and seven bowls (divine responses to false religions).

So what is the angel saying in Revelation 7? There are many more centuries of history still to come after AD 313 in which millions more will be saved and suffer death for Christ. Not till then will the saved be reaped. That is why we don't hear of the 144,000 again until seven chapters on, in chapter 14. Not until chapter 14 does the Lord Jesus put in his sickle and reap his wheat. In parables, the wheat always depicts the saved and the Lord is depicted as coming on a cloud with the souls of the saved in heaven to resurrect the living believers still on earth, as 1 Thessalonians 4:13–18 says.

What is the trademark of those believers? Revelation 14 tells you. They sing the new song! No unsaved person can sing that! They are those who have been redeemed.

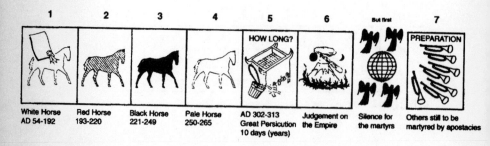

Fig. 26. Panel of the seven lampstands in Revelation's 'Arch of Triumph' depicting the seven Church periods of witness AD 96 to modern times.

Fig. 27. Panel of the seven seals in Revelation's 'Arch of Triumph' depicting Christ's triumph over three centuries of **Roman persecution**. AD 96 to AD 313. Note the symbol in seal 5 of prayers poured out, answered when the Roman Empire was Christianised.

Protection and deliverance

What a comforting picture for days like these. Today politicians openly talk of the possible destruction of all life on earth. Revelation 7 opens with a picture of our planet being threatened with destruction. This destruction is on land and sea and a third of trees are destroyed. But four angels hold back this threat until the number to be saved is completed. Our world is certainly threatened but it should comfort you to know that God reigns.

In the book of Revelation, there is a pattern – a structure. The whole wonderful book is unfolded upon this structure. For example, after each panel of sevens, God gives illustrations or parables to show what the panels mean. Each panel ends in triumph for Jesus Christ.

Now, a word about parables. You should always remember that parables are only given as illustrations. How are we to know the truth from error? Most errors are founded upon favourite interpretations of obscure symbols. They are not given to teach doctrine. For doctrine we read the clear statements of the epistles and Gospels.

36 TRIUMPHAL ARCH (1)

WARNING TRUMPETS

I was watching a pagentry of ancient warfare. The watchman on the city tower suddenly blew his trumpet. It was to warn the whole fortress that the enemy was coming. The defenders were surprised; they thought they had already defeated the enemy in an earlier battle. As the enemy advanced to attack the walls, the defenders tipped great iron bowls of scalding liquid upon them. One by one the bowls were poured out and the enemy retreated. This is the picture in the next three chapters of Revelation from 7 to 9. Seven angels prepare to sound the warning that the battle is not over.

We have seen how the seals of Revelation chapter 6 show a great victory. They depict how the Roman Empire was won over to accept Christianity by the fourth century. Christians rejoiced that the great battle of martyrdom was over. The battle seemed to be won. The whole population of the Empire was actually encouraged to go to church.

But heaven saw it differently. The seven angel trumpeters were to sound the warnings one by one. Satan was not going to be defeated as easily as that. The heathen now flooded into the church. As the centuries went by, their pagan ideas contaminated the truth. Christ offered the water of life; those waters were not poisoned, but chapter 8 verse 10 says a third of these waters were made bitter and many died.

Meanwhile, a fresh peril approaches as the next angel sounds his trumpet. This fifth trumpet was a peril which was to wipe out all the churches of North Africa (Rev 9).

You have probably guessed by now that the trumpets are warnings against false religion. Now look at our own churches.

Even in churches where the gospel is clearly preached, there are many who have never personally received Christ into their hearts as Saviour. It is as necessary to evangelise your own congregations as it is to evangelise the world.

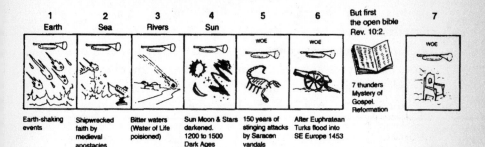

Fig. 28. The Panel of the seven trumpets.

THE TRUMPETS

We have seen how the fourth trumpet warned Christians of the Dark Ages, as they are called. Next, the fifth trumpet warned the church of the prophet of the desert – the false prophet which deceived many. It warned Christians of the Saracen invasion which was to sweep through Northern Africa and kill Christians and demolish the church.

The description of the devastating locusts of the fifth trumpet Dr Basil Atkinson identifies as the Saracen armies which swept like locusts out of Arabia about the year AD 613 and over-ran Syria, Egypt, Persia, North Africa and even into Spain.

The sixth trumpet was even a worse blow at Christendom, worse than the Saracen woe (Rev 9:12). The Euphratean power (the Turkish Empire) was unleashed in 1055 (v 12 onwards). This woe is symbolised by the River Euphrates. But the attack on European Christianity was to be held back for nearly 400 years, until the attack on Constantinople in 1453 (according to 9:15); Ezekiel said that each day in prophecy represents a year in history and the total of one year and one month and one day and one hour is therefore 396 years – or nearly 400 years.

This capital of Eastern Christianity fell because the Turks introduced gunpowder and cannon-fire. This is described in 9:17,18. At Istanbul today, you can see these ancient cannons displayed at the railway station. The gun muzzels were shaped like lions and the smoke of gunfire would belch out of their mouths when the cannon was fired, just as described in Revelation 9.

Verse 17 describes gunpowder very accurately fourteen centuries before it was invented. From out of the mouths of cannons 'issued fire, smoke and sulphur'. *The Oxford Dictionary* says, 'Gunpowder: an explosive of saltpetre, charcoal and sulphur'. The word in the Greek for smoke is *kaptos*, which the Greek lexicon defines as from the verb *kaptoo*, to burn to charcoal which gives off smoke. So 'fire, charcoal smoke, and sulphur' is a very close identification of the new military machine which fired at the walls of Constantinople (Istanbul), demolished them after 396 years' attempt, and broke through into south-east Europe. Its remnants can be seen today in conflicting ethnic areas in Yugoslavia.

The Ottoman military language is also described in these verses. They numbered their regiments by the term 'myriads' and this is the very word in the Greek of Revelation 9:16. This Turkish military word is used nowhere else in Scripture. Notice the description of these horsemen. They had breastplates of fiery colour, jacinth blue, and sulphur yellow. This was the well-known armour colour of the Turkish soldiers.

THE BIBLE REDISCOVERED

But Satan overstepped himself. The fall of Constantinople was a rebuke to the Church's idolatry, as God said, but it also caused the Greek Orthodox monks to flee to the West and bring with them the neglected Bible to be read and translated.

When the scholars of the Western Church began to translate them, they found a treasure beyond their wildest dreams. They could rejoice in a complete salvation accomplished by Christ on the cross. No longer did they have to whip themselves with metalled thongs, no longer did they have to wear prickly hair shirts in order to merit salvation. Christ had already saved them. He gave them abundant life as a free gift.

This next phase in Revelation 10:1 is represented by a mighty angel coming down from heaven with a rainbow around him, his face bright as the sun and a little book open in his hand. The Reformation indeed became the time of the open book. People were allowed to read it again.

CHECKPOINTS

SEVEN TRUMPETS AND SEVEN BOWLS

5th trumpet, Revelation 9:1–12
Saracens almost wipe out the great North African Church; vv 7–9 describe their famed horses, yellow turbans like crowns of gold, man-like beards, but woman-like long hair. Spiritual name (v 11) given in Hebrew because they overran Palestine, and in Greek because it was the Greek Orthodox Church which suffered.
Duration 150 years (5 mths v 5) AD 613–763 then settled.
Then another 150 years (v 10) AD 846–1096 of fresh attacks on North Mediterranean.

6th trumpet, Revelation 9:13–21. Second great woe, a worse blow to Christianity.

Turks launched their conquests from Baghdad in AD 1057. Restrained from SE Europe for 396 years (v 15) until 1453. Cannon and gunpowder (new weapon v 17) breached walls of Constantinople. (Gunpowder is made from chemicals of v 17 – saltpetre, charcoal and sulphur).
SE Europe subjugated. Monks flee to West with old Scriptures.
Reformation, chapter 10. Translations from old Scriptures bring an open Bible recommission.
'A little book open' 'Take it . . . preach again to the nations.'

Cauldrons (bowls of wrath) reverse the trumpet apostacies

Reply to 1st Apostacy of Trumpets 1–4 and 2nd Apostacy 5.6.
Angel of the cauldrons shows John the meaning of everything
from
Chapters 15 to 22 (cf. Rev 17:1; 21:9; 22:1).
The false bride in red claiming to be the Church (chaps 17 to 19:4).
The true bride in white (19:5–9).
The return of her groom, the King of Kings (19:11–18).
The two apostacies finally demolished (vv 19–21).
Satan chained during millennium (20:1–3).
Christ's reign for 1,000 years.
Final Judgement Day (20:11–15; Jn 5:29).
The Bride's heaven (21:9–22:17).
The Bride's invitation to the wedding (22:17).

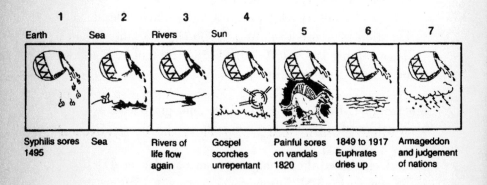

Fig. 29. Panel of the seven bowls in Revelation's 'Arch of Triumph' depicting replies of the bowls to each trumpet AD 1500 to the End. (Mainly to do with apostasy and response to false religions.)

CHECKPOINTS

THE NEXT CENTURY

The Rapture

- Illustrated in Revelation is the first resurrection. Those who believed.

  The wheat harvest in spring – Christ's wheat are those who die in the Lord (Rev 14:13–16).

  The grapes and fruit harvest in autumn is the second resurrection, i.e. The ungodly for judgement (14:17–20; 20:5, 11–15 [cf. 1 Cor 15:25–26]).

  One of the plagues was destructive Bible criticism (15:3). Victory was gained over them by those who sang the song of Moses and the Lamb, i.e. Moses' writings were genuine and the Lamb's atonement fully effective (says Dr Basil Atkinson).

- Rapture is next illustrated in 16:15 before Armageddon in v 16 (cf. Is 26:19–21).

  'I am coming like a thief' This simile is used 5 times:

  1. Revelation 16:15.
  2. Matthew 24:43 'Shall gather his elect'.
  3. 1 Thessalonians 5:2. Children of light should not be surprised (vv 4,5).
  4. 2 Peter 3:10. 'Be blameless' (v 14).
  5. Revelation 3:3 Unworthy Christians warned as in 1 Cor 3:8–15.

- Rapture next mentioned in 20:6 'This is the first resurrection' (cf. 1 Pet 4:17).

The Millennium Revelation 20:2–7.

- When? Opinion not essential. Love is more important (1 Cor 13:2)
- Pointers:
  1. Kingdom comes after Christ's return (Lk 21:31: Zech 14:9–12; Joel 3:12–18; Hab 2:14; Dan 7:13–14).
  2. Peace in creation follows Christians resurrection (Rom 8:19–23).

3. Described in other scriptures, 1 and 2 Peter, 'age-lasting day' of 1,000 years.
   Isaiah 2:2–4; Micah 4:1–8. Wars cease (Is 11:6–9; 65:17–25). Peace among animals.
4. Before Christ's return, things get worse not better (2 Tim 3:13; Lk 21:34–36; Mt 24:12; 2 Thess 2:3–8).

37 Triumphal Arch (2)

FUTURISTIC APPLICATION

In the closing chapters of Revelation, we see a marvellous future, but before we look at that, we will sum up the traumatic past which leads to that wonderful time ahead for the Christians.

Someone said, 'If there is one thing men learn from history, it is that men never learn from history!' What Christianity doesn't learn from history is not to have divisions over non-essentials such as whether the book of Revelation is in the past or in the future.

The book of Revelation opens by predicting the history of Christian witness. That is the first panel of seven lampstands, the triumphs and failures of the Church. Then follow the usual visions explaining the meaning. These show that history is in the hands of Jesus, the Lamb of God, and that he triumphs.

The second panel of sevens – that of the seals – is the history of how the blood of the martyrs eventually won the Roman Empire to accept Christianity by the fourth century. The visions that follow show that the prayers and suffering of Christians were thus answered, but there are perils to come from other quarters.

The third panel is of seven trumpet warnings that the enemy Satan is advancing to attack the citadel of truth in a more subtle guise – that of false religions. The pagan priests who flooded into the churches were not really converted and brought in with them practices which originated from Babylon. The water of life was thus poisoned under the third trumpet, and under the fourth trumpet, the light of truth was obscured; verse 12 says, 'darkened'. These were the Dark Ages, an appropriate name.

Then under the fifth trumpet in the seventh century, comes the attack from the false prophet of the desert. The Saracen invasion wiped out the churches of North Africa during 150 years.

The actual duration was foretold. But Satan oversteps himself for under the sixth trumpet the Turks break into south-east Europe in 1453. This causes the Reformation because the refugee monks brought the Bible to the West and, when translated, it became the open Bible of the Reformation (Rev 10).

The fourth and last panel shows how the bowls of anger are poured out upon unscriptural error. These purify the contaminated waters to bring life eternal and the sunlight of the gospel shines once again. Under the sixth bowl, the Turkish Empire dries up from Europe and Palestine. It does so in the time scale accurately indicated, so that God's purposes are fulfilled in his Holy Land before the second coming of Christ. For this reason Hitler died as he would have destroyed the State of Israel and Britain declined because she blocked the return of the Jews after the war. Technology has advanced so rapidly recently that a futuristic literal fulfilment of the symbols of Revelation will soon be possible.

JUSTICE FOR ALL

The destiny of all life is justice and fairness for all. This is because the Creator is just and good. The Bible makes this quite clear, a happy world as God originally intended will be restored, but this will require just judgement. A just and happy world was sidetracked by man's rebellion, but as we see in Romans 8:19–23 the animal kingdom will be at peace in the millennium. This accords with Isaiah 65:25 where there will be no more predators: ' "The wolf and the lamb shall graze together, and the lion shall eat straw like the ox; and dust shall be the serpent's food. They shall do no evil or harm in my Holy mountain" says the LORD'.

Justice will be done in the human race also. 'Everyone will give an account of the deeds done while he was alive whether they were good or bad.' Many scriptures repeat this. No one will be able to say that the sentence at judgement day will be not correctly deserved. Good deeds will be rightly rewarded. Wickedness will be properly punished. You would not like child torturers to escape would you? You would not like the Hitlers and cruel murderers to escape because the police have failed to find them? "Everyone will give an account before God, 'I saw the dead stand before God, great and small' and everyone was judged according to their deeds good or bad". Compare the following scriptures: Acts 17:31; 2 Corinthians 5:10 and Revelation 20: 11–15. But what about hell fire? Fire burns up rubbish. There will be a clean universe.

> The picture of wonderful bliss and happiness comes in the last two chapters of the Bible only after all evil has been destroyed in the two earlier chapters. Hell is the rubbish pit in which all evil has been burnt after just sentences have been implemented followed by the Second Death. Jesus referred to this when he encouraged his disciples to face physical death through witnessing for him. He said "Don't be afraid of those who can kill your bodies but are unable to kill your soul, but rather fear God who is able to kill both soul and body in hell' (Matthew 10:28).

Mercy not Justice

But one may say, 'My life has not been all that good so its mercy I need not justice. I need forgiveness not deserts.' For God to forgive is a problem. He can forgive justly because he is the just upholder of the universe and another had to suffer your punishment – the Lord Jesus Christ who has never sinned. The good news is that you are forgiven the moment you accept what he has done for you. That is why the Bible ends with this wonderful invitation: 'The Spirit and the bride say come, and him who hears always come, and him who hears says coame. And he who is thirsty come. And whoever will let him take the water of life freely.'.

SUMMATION

So this marvellous insight demonstrates how history is in the hands of the Lamb of God. He opens each page of traumatic history and he triumphs over Satan at each main stage. Finally, the kingdom of this world becomes the Kingdom of God and of his Christ.

The final curtain rises on a new heaven and a new earth wherein dwells righteousness and joy and the redeemed radiate the iridescent light streaming from the Father and the Son. All faithful believers will also triumph with him and sing, 'Salvation belongs to our God who sits upon the throne and unto the Lamb . . . Worthy is the Lamb who has redeemed us out of every tribe and family and nation . . . Hallelujah, the Lord God, the Almighty reigns.'

CHECKPOINTS

THE FUTURISTIC INTERPRETATION

Futuristic application of panels 2-4 (seals, trumpets and cauldrons)
Prophecy often fulfilled both ways (Mt 17:10–13).
They are to be re-enacted literally during the Tribulation (i.e. during seven years between Rapture and Judgement of nations).
Science of destruction has now made it possible (i.e. devastation through chemical, germal and nuclear warfare).
Appearance of anti-christ, world government and multi-faith Elijah comes literally (Rev 11:3,6). In John the Baptist it was spiritually fulfilled (Mt 17:13).

A great delusion
Satan deceives the whole world (Rev 12:9; 19:20; 20:3,10).
Turning to myths in the last days (2 Tim 4:4; 2 Thess 2:9–11; 2 Pet 3:3–7).
Anthropologists admit no evidence of any stooping ape-men period
- 'Still to find evidence of very first bi-pedal apes' R.L. 1992 (yet he draws pictures of stooping ape-men).
- 'We have no fossils yet to tell us of the in between time' D.J. ('but we can picture it,' he says).
- 'This fossil void is particularly frustrating' M.P. (but he assumes that it happened).
- Dubois 1880, hid leg bones of early man for 20 years (which proved upright walking).

Lessons from Revelation irrespective of interpretation
> Glory of Jesus unveiled.
> Inspires worship and Christian songs.
> We see the redeemed enjoying their salvation.
> The Lamb controls history.
> Love story of the Bride and Christ concluded.

38 HOW THE SECOND COMING WILL AFFECT YOU

Now that you have been thrilled by the insights into prophecy, you will want to know how it will happen.

First, I will describe how it will affect you by the main facts which all are agreed on. Then we will look at the other details which others are not so sure about. I find that often they can be clearly analysed from a humble and consistent examination of the Bible.

YOUR SEAT ON THE BENCH

What then is the clear factor which will make great changes to everybody's life? It is the statement that Jesus Christ will descend from heaven with great power and glory suddenly to judge the living and the dead. He will also judge the nations and everyone will have to give an account of his deeds.

So, if you accept Christ's salvation, there is a wonderful tomorrow for you. 'Do you not know that the saints will judge the world and if the world will be judged by you, are you unworthy to judge even the smallest of matters' (1 Cor 6:2).

You may remark, 'But am I a saint? Do I qualify?' In the New Testament, the word 'saint' is used for a person who has accepted the free salvation of Christ.

So you see, a saint is a forgiven and cleansed sinner and as such, you will be with that triumphant host of saints and angels who descend from heaven to Jerusalem.

ON EARTH AS IT IS IN HEAVEN

What is your answer to those who say to you, 'Why does God

allow all this suffering, injustice and violence?' I find the best answer is that one day soon the Lord is going to show the kind of earth he originally intended. That is after his return to reign.

The events after this are given in Scripture but some are not sure about the order. That is not so important as the fact that they will happen. I believe, however, that a careful correlation of scriptures sorts out the following details:

Christ descends to judge the nations. (Mt 25:31,32; Dan 2:44 and 7:13).

The saved with their new bodies will descend with him (Daniel 7:24–27) and set up a just and happy rule upon earth of 1,000 years called the millennium. This millennium is described by nine writers in over twelve places in the Old and New Testament – by Paul: 1 Corinthians 15:23–27 and Romans 8:19–23; by Daniel in chapter 7:13,14,27; by Isaiah in 2:1–5; 11:6–9; 65:17–25; by Ezekiel 48:35; by Joel 3:12–18; by Zechariah 14:16–21; and by John in Revelation 20:4–6.

EARLY FATHERS AGREE

All the Early Fathers of the first four centuries agree that the millennium follows Christ's coming. Papias, St John's disciple, says John taught it, and that the judgement of the unsaved will come at the end of the millennium (Rev 20:5,11–15). Believers will not appear at this (Jn 5:24,29).

Finally the universe will be cleaned up and the whole kingdom delivered up to the Father (1 Cor 15:27,28; Rev 21:27 to 22:5) and the Bible story ends with praise and joy and an invitation to you to be in that grand new world, and to be part of that destiny towards which all life is moving.

CHECKPOINTS

THE ORDER OF EVENTS TO COME

- **The Rapture.** Believers alive or dead will be caught up to meet Christ in the air, with changed bodies, (2 Thess 2:1: 1 Thess 4:17,17; 1 Cor 15:51,54).
- **The Bride** (believers) married to the Saviour as in Matthew 25. The order then gives:
- **The reward-giving** (Mt 25:14–30) called Christ's judgement seat or Bema (2 Cor 5:10).
- **Descent of believers** with Christ to judge the nations (Mt 25:31,32; Dan 7:18; 1 Cor 6:2).
- **Christ and the believers** will establish a happy and just millennium (1 Cor 15:23,27; Dan 7:13,14,27; Is 2:1–5; Zech 14:9–21; Rev 20:5,6).
- **Millennium ends.** Unsaved dead raised for judgement (Jn 5:29; Rev 20:5,11–15).
- **Whole universe cleaned** up and delivered to the Father (1 Cor 15:27,28; Rev 21:1,5,6).
- **The eternal heavenly state** of purity, goodness and joy emanating from the Creator.

CONCLUSION

The universe began by being created good in Genesis chapter 1, but sin and rebellion spoilt it. The creative Word, Jesus Christ redeemed it and us, so the Bible ends in Revelation with a new eternal heavenly state of joy and goodness which radiates with the divine source of all light.

Current events in Europe and the Middle East indicate that the return of the Lord draws near.

It is a privilege to know that we can belong to Christ to fulfil his purposes in our lives in these significant days.

GLOSSARY OF TERMS

Age-day Theory That Genesis days were an age or a great long period was held by the original founders of Creation Science.

Anthropic Principle That the beginning of the universe shows that man was its object, now held by a majority of scientists.

Assyriology Archaeological research in Assyria (now North Iraq).

Astrophysics Study of physics and chemistry of heavenly bodies.

Big Bang Theory That the universe had a beginning in an explosion of primary elements, as opposed to Steady State theory which thought there was no beginning.

Centresomes A mechanism in the cell which draws each duplicate chromosome into the newly-forming cell.

Chromosome Each cell contains chromosomes which contain the instructions for making and sustaining an animal or plant. It is a double helical ribbon upon which instructions are recorded in code.

Cosmology Science of the universe.

DNA Short for Deoxyribonucleic Acid, the material of which genes and chromosomes are made.

Diploid Both ends of an axis.

Genes Are the smallest sections in the DNA instructions.

JEDP Jehovah, Elokim, Deuteronomy, Priestly. Supposed sources from which it was conjectured that the Old Testament was compiled. Archaeology has since found that the ancients did not piece together literature in this way.

M RNA Messenger Ribonucleic Acid. It is a copy of a section of DNA which the messenger takes to the ribosome production machines in the cell.

Meson An unstable particle.

Mitochondrion The independent organelle in the cell which manufactures fuel to run the cell's machinery.

Neutron A particle in an atom without a positive or negative charge.

Proton A positively charged particle in an atom. How many these are determines the material's nature.

Quark The basic building block of all atomic particles.

Ribosomes The machines in the cell which decode the M RNA instructions and assemble protein chains of body parts as instructed.

Year-day prophecy Certain prophecies use numbers in which days represent years as in Ezekiel 4:6.